PLAYING BY THE RULES

The Rules of Golf, Explained & Illustrated

From a Lifetime in the Game

ARNOLD PALMER

POCKET
BOOKS

New York • London • Toronto • Sydney

To having fun and enjoying the game of golf

ACKNOWLEDGMENTS

No book about the rules of golf could possibly be written without the help of experts. This one is no exception. I would like to thank Jeff Hall and David Fay of the USGA, as well as my dear friends, John Staver and Buzz Taylor, who volunteered their time and expertise to make this book as accurate as possible. Any mistakes in these pages are mine, not theirs.

Also, I'd like to thank my publisher and friend, Judith Curr, for her belief in this book and her patience and hard work in making it a reality. To my friends, Steve Eubanks and Doc Giffin, I offer my heartfelt thanks for all your efforts; and to my long-time associates at IMG, Mark H. McCormack, Alastair Johnston, Bev Norwood, and Mark Reiter, I am deeply indebted.

The biggest thanks of all goes out to all the golfers out there who have had or who will have quirky, head-scratching rules questions. Without you, this book would mean nothing.

Thanks, and enjoy the book and the game.

PLAYING BY THE RULES

I was playing a round of golf with some friends recently when one of my partners brought up a highly publicized incident he'd seen on television.

"Arnie," he said, "how on earth did Ian Woosnam end up with fifteen clubs in his bag at the British Open?"

"Happens more than you think," I said. "You're on the range fooling around with different clubs and you walk to the tee with too many in your bag. Of course, most of the time your caddie counts clubs before you tee off and you catch the mistake before it costs you two shots."

"Has it ever happened to you?" my friend wanted to know.

"No, I always check the bag myself. Ian relied on his caddie, and the caddie let him down."

"So, what if the caddie had kept his mouth shut? Could they have played the whole round without anybody finding out? And what if they'd played more than one hole? How big would the penalty have been then?"

Before I could answer those questions, another member of our group joined the discussion. "Who came up with the idea of only fourteen clubs anyway?" he said. "Why not fifteen, or sixteen, or twelve?"

Finally I threw my hands up, and we all had a good laugh.

Questions like that come up all the time in my foursome, but I'm not alone. Every day at golf courses all over the world questions about the rules of golf are being asked and debated in locker rooms and on the first tees and, as was the case with my friends, one question usually sparks two or three more.

I've played competitive golf for over half a century now, and I still love it as much today as I did as a child growing up in Latrobe, Pennsylvania. But even after all these years playing thousands of competitive rounds, I still run across new and fascinating nuances in the rules of golf. As much golf as I've played over the years, you would think I had seen every head-scratching, eyebrow-raising, stranger-than-fiction rule scenario there is, but every so often a situation comes along that leaves me saying, "Hmm, I wonder how that's handled under the rules." That's one of the reasons I thought a book about golf rulings—the quirky situations that have come up over the years and how they were handled by golf's ruling bodies—would make an interesting read.

Heaven knows I've also been involved in enough controversial rulings in my own career. Some of my more highly publicized and controversial rules situations continue to be debated in grill rooms around the world forty to fifty years after the fact, while other rulings I've been involved in barely warrant the attention of the professional staff at Latrobe Country Club (where I play most of my summer golf) or the Bay Hill Club in Orlando where I spend most of my winters. Still I'm asked about various rulings, with friends and acquaintances saying things like, "Arnie, that drop you took in the U.S. Open back in such-and-so year, what was the situation there again?" or "Arnie, didn't you have a penalty in this-or-that tournament for breaking rule whatever?"

From what I've seen over the years, golfers don't have a passing interest in the rules of the game: They are obsessed by the rules. Just look at the number of phone calls and e-mails the PGA Tour receives regarding rulings. A golf fan at home turns on the television and sees what he thinks is a violation of the rules, and he immediately calls the tournament director to report it. With so much golf on television these days, that sort of thing happens almost every week now. Sometimes the fans are right. Sometimes the pros make mistakes that are caught by the camera. But most of the time the golf fans watching at home are just like the average golfers in my foursome or in foursomes all over the country: They know just enough about the rules to be dangerous.

It should be easy. There are only thirty-four rules in our game—fewer than baseball, basketball, football, soccer, rugby, and cricket—and the rule book is available to anyone who wants it. You don't have to be an umpire or official to own a copy of the *Rules of Golf* as published by the USGA or the Royal and Ancient Golf Club of St. Andrews. In fact, most golf shops have several versions lying around, and anyone who has a question can ask his local pro.

But not every rules situation is simple and straightforward. Golf is a game of only thirty-four rules but a million variables. Average golfers can't be expected to know all the scenarios in the game. Most touring pros don't know everything there is to know about the rules. The USGA give rules seminars around the country to educate and inform the golfing public about the rules, but even rules officials can make some bad rulings in the heat of the moment.

The truth is, nobody's perfect. Tour pros make mistakes, rules officials sometimes make mistakes, and average golfers playing leisurely rounds on Saturday mornings with their buddies make mistakes. It's the nature of the game. But it's also the nature of the game for golfers to do everything in their power to rectify their mistakes and play the game in accordance with the rules.

Golf has always been, and hopefully will always remain, a gentleman's game. Thousands of rounds are played every day at country clubs, resorts, and public courses around the world without benefit of umpires, referees, judges, or officials. The rules of our game fascinate us because we are our own umpires. Golfers are self-policing, regularly calling penalties on themselves for rules infractions like carrying too many clubs. Why did Ian Woosnam's caddie tell his boss about the 15th club in the bag? Because it would never occur to him to do anything else. The integrity of the game is more important than any single tournament or any one player, and everyone who plays our game does so under that same code of honor.

Rules and rulings in golf are what make our sport unique. The fan sitting at home can relate to the penalty stroke a tour pro is taking for hitting his ball into a water hazard, because average golfers incur those same penalties every day.

Just as players and rules officials make occasional mistakes, the rules themselves aren't perfect either. The rule book wasn't handed down by the Almighty on stone tablets. It's written by men and women who love the game. Those men and women also edit and revise the rules every four years, making subtle changes to reflect any situations that might have occurred in which the existing rulings were vague or fuzzy. Some of the examples I've used in this book prompted changes in the rules in their time, and others will likely be debated in future meetings of golf's ruling bodies.

In presenting this book to you, I hope to make certain golf rulings clearer and provide you with a practical interpretation of why certain rules work the way they do. By going down memory lane with me, rehashing some famous and some not-so-famous rulings, hopefully you will gain a better understanding of how and why the rules of golf work the way they do. Hopefully the lessons you learn will help you enjoy the game.

If I'm successful on that front—if anything you pick up in these pages makes the game a little more fun—then the time and effort that has gone into this book will have been worth it.

Enjoy perusing the rules and rulings, but more importantly, go out and enjoy the game.

The Game

The first rule in the rule book is a simple one, but one that is broken more often than it's obeyed, which is hard to believe considering it's so straightforward. The first section of the rule—**Rule 1-1**—reads:

> **The Game of Golf consists in playing a ball from the teeing ground into the hole by a stroke or successive strokes in accordance with the Rules.**

You would think that would be simple enough. It's a general definition of the game that everyone, even those who don't play golf, knows and recognizes. You start golf by hitting a ball from the tee into the hole in the fewest strokes possible under the rules. You hit it, find it, and hit it again, until you get it in the hole. You can't mess this rule up, right?

Wrong. Anytime you're playing in a stroke play competition, and you concede a putt, you've broken this rule. The rule states that you have to play "from the teeing ground into the hole," not "from the teeing ground to a spot close to the hole where everyone knows you'd make it anyway." Kicking a two-inch putt back to someone in a stroke play event, or saying, "That's good, pick it up," to a fellow competitor is a violation of this rule, one that occurs every day in clubs all over the world.

This is where the vagaries between match play (which is defined in Rule 2 of the rule book) and stroke play (which is covered by Rule 3) confuse the average player. In match play, you can certainly concede a putt or a hole. Since match play is a game between two competitors or two teams of competitors, one player or one team can certainly "give" a putt to another, whether to concede the hole or simply to move things along at a reasonable pace.

One of the most famous examples of this occurred in the 1969 Ryder Cup Matches at Royal Birkdale in Southport, England. The Great Britain and Ireland team was still a little miffed by the remarks U.S. Captain Ben Hogan had made prior to the 1967 Matches in Houston, Texas. I was on that team, sitting a few feet from Hogan at the gala dinner when he made the introductions. Dai Rees, the venerable captain of the GB&I team, introduced each player by giving an elegant speech that enticed everyone to applaud. Hogan then stood up and called for quiet, saying his speech would be much shorter. "Ladies and gentlemen," Hogan said, motioning toward those of us on the U.S. side of the table, "the best golfers in the world." Then he sat down.

Boy, the Britons were hot about that one. We beat the GB&I team 23½ points to 8½ points that year, a real trouncing, which didn't help matters. When the matches went back across the pond to Southport, the lingering sting from Hogan's introduction still plagued them.

The GB&I team played better than they had in years, knotting the matches at 15½ points apiece on the final day. It all came down to a final singles match between Tony Jacklin and Jack Nicklaus. Jacklin had been one down with two to play, but made an eagle at the par-five 17th to square the match. At the 18th, Nicklaus barely missed a birdie putt, but tapped in for par. Jacklin was left with a two-footer to halve the hole and the match, thus insuring a tie in the Ryder Cup. The Ryder Cup matches had never ended in a tie, but Nicklaus made history that afternoon by picking up Jacklin's marker and conceding the putt, in essence saying to Jacklin, "That's good."

Walking off the green, Nicklaus said to Jacklin, "I don't think you would have missed that, Tony, but under the circumstances I'd never give you the opportunity."

Jack has been criticized over the years for that concession. J. C. Snead still seethes when the subject is brought up. "It wasn't the Jack Nicklaus Cup," Snead says. "It was the Ryder Cup. Jack had no right to give that putt when his other teammates had no say in the matter."

That's where J. C. is wrong. Under the rules of match play, Jack had every right to concede the putt, because, while both players were part of larger teams, the match was between Nicklaus and Jacklin. Under the rules of golf, Jack had every right to do what he did.

Confusion about Rule 1 comes in stroke play competitions that range from the tournaments we play week-in and week-out on the PGA and PGA Senior Tours, to the club championships and Wednesday dogfights that are held every week at courses all over America. In those tournaments there are more than two people competing and more than one group to consider. If you give a putt to one of the guys in your foursome, it adversely affects the fellow competitors who aren't in your group, and who might take umbrage with your generosity. In stroke play situations, the definition of the game in Rule 1-1 means what it says. You have to play from the teeing ground into the hole with no given putts. If you pick up a two-incher, you haven't played the game.

I even got confused by this rule once in a U.S. Open. It was 1962 and I was coming into the summer having had a pretty good year. I'd won the Masters, the Bob Hope Desert Classic, the Phoenix Open, the Texas Open, and the Tournament of Champions before returning home to Pennsylvania for our national championship at Oakmont Country Club in suburban Pittsburgh. I was certainly favored to win that year. Oakmont is only an hour's drive from my home in Latrobe, and I was coming into the event playing as well as I ever had since turning pro. But 13 three-putt greens in the course of 72 holes blew my chances. Still, I had an eight-footer on the 72nd hole to win the golf tournament, but as had happened too often during the week, I felt like I was putting with a wet noodle out there. The putt to win never had a chance and I finished tied for the lead at the end of regulation.

The following day, a Sunday, Jack Nicklaus and I went back to the course for an 18-hole playoff to determine the winner of the

1962 U.S. Open. Jack had shot a 69 in the fourth round to tie me with an aggregate score of 283, and his putting had been a hundred times better than mine had been all week.

My putting woes continued throughout the playoff. Finally, on the 18th, Jack led by two shots. I needed to make an eagle if Jack made a par, and the way he had played all day there was no doubt in my mind that par was the worst score he would make. I didn't make eagle, or birdie, or even par. When I tapped in for bogey and Jack rolled his birdie putt to within three inches, it was obviously over. In a gesture of concession, I picked up Jack's marker and tossed it back to him, shaking his hand and congratulating him on winning his first U.S. Open Championship.

But there was a problem. Joe Dey, our rules official, informed us that I couldn't concede the putt. This was a stroke play competition and Jack had to finish in order to be declared the winner.

I was confused. There were only two people in the playoff, so there weren't any other competitors to consider. The rest of the field had finished the day before, and Jack and I were the only golfers anywhere in sight. One of us would win, and the other would finish second. Jack had obviously beaten me, and I had done what I considered the honorable thing by conceding the last putt.

Even so, U.S. Open playoffs are stroke play events, not match play events. Jack had to start from the teeing ground and knock his ball in the hole in order for the victory to count. He replaced his ball, and rolled in the three-inch putt to win.

Jack seemed happy with my concession at the U.S. Open, although it turned out to be against the rules. Putts can't be conceded in stroke play, even when only two of you are playing. ARNOLD PALMER'S PERSONAL COLLECTION

The other three sub-sections of Rule 1 have also caused their fair share of controversies over the years. The second part of the rule—**Rule 1-2**—reads:

> **No player or caddie shall take any action to in-fluence the position or the movement of a ball except in accordance with the Rules.**

No kicking or rolling or nudging your ball out of a divot and into a better lie, and no fudging the position of the ball with your club. Your caddie can't pick up your ball, clean it, then perch it on a tuft of grass near its original position. Nor can your caddie swat an errant shot of yours back into play, or kick a ball that's rolling toward the water. All those things are illegal under the rules and subject to penalties ranging from two shots for a minor infraction to disqualification if you're caught blatantly cheating.

The most famous incident involving this rule occurred in the 1946 U.S. Open. On the par-five 15th hole at Canterbury Golf Club in Cleveland during the third round, Byron Nelson hit his second shot in the gallery to the right. Nelson's caddie, a young man named Eddie Martin, ducked under the gallery rope the marshals were holding for him, but the ropes were so close to the ball that Martin inadvertently kicked Nelson's ball, moving it about a foot. After a lengthy conference with USGA official Ike Grainger, Nelson was assessed a two-shot penalty. That proved to be the turning point in the tournament. Nelson finished tied with Lloyd Mangrum, and lost that U.S. Open in an 18-hole playoff. Two months later, Nelson retired from competitive golf.

A more recent and far more controversial testing of Rule 1-2 occurred in 1997 at the LPGA's Corning Classic. Looking for her first win, Sweden's Carin Koch led in the third round when she hooked her tee shot on the 16th into some pine trees adjacent to the driving range. After a frantic search by gallery members and officials, Koch assumed her ball was lost, so she trotted back to the tee to hit another ball. On her way back her caddie, who was also her husband, Stephan, told Carin he had seen her original ball fall from one of the trees. Carin came back, identified the ball, and played it from the left rough.

The other caddie in the group, Robert Klasson, who was working for Charlotta Sorenstam, claimed that Stephan had shaken the tree to dislodge the ball. Stephan denied the charge, and LPGA official Angus Mackenzie sided with the Kochs, citing no firm evidence that Stephan had done anything to influence the position of the ball. "It's one person's word against another's," Mackenzie said. "We gave Carin the benefit of the doubt and let her proceed as if the ball was in play."

The following day, Klasson came forward with a couple of spectators who said they too had seen Stephan Koch shake the tree and dislodge the ball. Even though none of the tour officials who had aided in the search for Carin's ball had seen anything untoward, LPGA officials assessed Koch a two-shot penalty based on the testimony of the elderly couple who claimed to have been in the gallery, then disqualified her for signing an incorrect scorecard.

"It's as though they accused us of cheating," Koch said later, still bitter about the whole ordeal. "I tried to block the whole thing out of my mind, but when someone calls your husband a liar, it's hard."

Koch redeemed herself in 2001 when, in her first trip back to Corning since the incident, she won the Corning Classic and put the rules incident behind her for good.

The third section of **Rule 1**—**Rule 1-3**—is probably the most broken rule in the entire rule book. It reads:

Byron Nelson's 1946 U.S. Open didn't end well after his caddie accidentally kicked Byron's ball. The penalty cost Byron the championship.
ASSOCIATED PRESS/AP

Players shall not agree to exclude the operation of any Rule or to waive any penalty incurred.

That means you can't agree ahead of time to break the rules, which everyone does at some point. If you stand on the first tee and say, "Okay, guys, we're rolling it in the fairway today and all putts in the leather are good," you've broken Rule 1-3.

Carin Koch and her husband, Stephan, weren't happy to be disqualified from the Corning Classic, but they came back as a team to win the tournament later. ASSOCIATED PRESS/AP

I break it at least once a week. At Bay Hill we have a game we call the shootout. It's an 18-hole tournament we play almost every day. But before anybody tees off they know that the rule limiting you to 14 clubs (Rule 4-4) has been waived. I usually have between 15 and 18 clubs in my bag, depending on how many drivers and putters I want to try that day, while some guys carry three or four wedges and three or four woods to go with the standard complement of irons. It's a clear and flagrant violation of the rules, and we all know it. But we've agreed to break the rule, thus violating Rule 1-3.

We also have mulligans on the first tee, another flagrant violation—one we have all agreed to ahead of time. But I don't know a club in the country that doesn't have similar games with similar agreements. That makes Rule 1-3 the most violated rule in all of golf.

The final section of **Rule 1** is the catch-all rule, which outlines what happens in situations not covered by the rules as they exist. It reads:

> **If any point in dispute is not covered by the Rules, the decision shall be made in accordance with equity.**

It's commonly called the "rule of equity," and in my humble opinion, this rule isn't used enough when situations of fairness

Tim Simpson was delighted to escape without penalty or injury after hitting his ball near an alligator in my Bay Hill Invitational. ASSOCIATED PRESS/AP

are at stake (a subject I'll get into in more detail later), but it is a good one to have for all those situations the rules don't anticipate.

In my tournament, the Bay Hill Invitational, we were faced with an unusual situation that required the rule of equity. It was 1988, and Tim Simpson and Raymond Floyd were playing together on Saturday when Tim hooked his ball near a water hazard on the third hole. As the two players walked over to where Tim's ball had stopped, they were alarmed to see a ten-foot alligator sunning on the bank. Inches from the alligator's mouth lay Tim's ball.

Mark Russell, a PGA Tour rules official, was quickly dispatched to assess the situation, and after a couple of minutes of discussing the relative dangers of approaching an alligator of that size, Russell allowed Tim to put another ball in play in a safe spot not nearer the hole. The officials made that ruling because it was the only right and equitable thing to do.

Tim didn't win my tournament that year, but he didn't get eaten by a reptile either.

Match Play

and

Stroke Play

The next two rules, Rules 2 and 3, outline and define the two most common types of games in golf: stroke play and match play competitions.

The majority of the games played at clubs across the country are match play contests, which are defined by Rule 2 in the rule book. In your group, you and one of your buddies might play the other two players in a four-ball nassau, and if you and your partner win the first hole you go "one up" in accordance with the scoring procedures for match play. It doesn't matter if your score is a bogey and your opponent's score is a double bogey, you still win the hole, just as if you had made double eagle. You gain the same advantage in match play when you win the hole by one shot as you do when you win it by three shots. You're still only one hole up, or, more commonly, "one up."

If you and your partner lose the first hole, you're "one down," and if both teams tie the first hole, the hole is said to have been "halved" and the match is "all square." This is how most recreational golf is played in America. It's also how many of the old amateur and professional tournaments were contested. The PGA Championship was match play until the 1950s, and the U.S. Amateur, British Amateur, and North and South Amateur championships are still contested under match play.

But touring pros don't see match play much anymore. Most professional tournaments these days are stroke play contests (as defined in Rule 3) in which each player is competing against the other 100 or so other players in the field. At the end of the tournament, the player with the lowest score wins.

About the only match play events the clubs have (other than the games they get at their home courses or the Tuesday and Wednesday practice matches they set up with fellow pros) are the Accenture WGC Match Play Championship, the Ryder Cup, the President's Cup, and the Cisco World Match Play Championships in England. None of those events have a full field of players, so it's reasonable to say that a majority of professional golfers rarely ever compete in match play tournaments.

The different formats confuse some players. During the inaugural Accenture Match Play Championship in Carlsbad, California, there was more than a little confusion about how the event was being scored. After walking off the 18th green of their Thursday match, Steve Pate, who had beaten Davis Love III one-up, looked around for the scoring trailer, a staple on the PGA Tour where all scores must be tallied and all cards signed and attested. "What do we do now?" Pate asked.

Love glanced around, looking for the trailer, then pulled the scorecard from his back pocket.

"You have a scorecard?" Pate asked.

"Yeah," Love said, "but I don't know what to do with it."

"I don't know either," Pate said, and the two of them stood around until an official came by and told them the match had already been officially recorded as a one-up victory for Pate.

There are other vagaries between match play and stroke play, but the biggest difference is the type of penalty incurred for a rules infraction. All penalties in stroke play are either one or two shots, or, in more severe cases, disqualification. Match play penalties can be a shot for things like lost balls or relief from water hazards, but other violations can result in "loss of hole" penalties.

Rule 2-6 reads:

> **The penalty for a breach of a Rule in match play is loss of hole except when otherwise provided.**

In the 1999 USGA Senior Women's Amateur at Desert Mountain Golf Club in Scottsdale, Arizona, local Scottsdale resident Betsy Bro lost a semifinal match on the 19th hole when she inadvertently picked up her opponent's ball. Under match play rules the mistake cost Bro one shot. Because the match was tied at the end of the regulation and the players were in sudden death overtime, the penalty cost Bro the match.

"It makes me sad," she said afterward. "It was a technicality. We were both playing the same ball and both had black dots on them, but she had more dots on hers than I had on mine. All of us assumed it was my ball. But that's what happens. We were so careful all week to follow the rules, but there are rules of golf. I'm just sorry it ended like that."

I will almost guarantee you Bro will never break that rule again.

The other major difference between match play and stroke play as outlined in Rules 2 and 3 are the way claims or disputes are settled. **Rule 2-5** states in part:

> **In match play, if a doubt or dispute arises between the players and no duly authorized representative of the Committee is available within a reasonable time, the players shall continue the match without delay. Any claim, if it is to be considered by the Committee, must be made before any player in the match plays from the next teeing ground ...**

In other words, if you think your opponent broke a rule, you can't wait three or four holes to make your claim.

In stroke play, if you're in doubt as to a procedure or a rule, you can always play a second ball and ask an official for a ruling. The wording of this rule is:

> **Rule 3-3a: Procedure**
> **In stroke play only, when during play of a hole a competitor is doubtful of his rights or procedure, he may, without penalty, play a second ball. After the situation which caused the doubt has arisen, the competitor should, before taking further action, announce to his marker or a fellow-competitor his decision to invoke this Rule and the ball with which he will score if the Rules permit.**

Perhaps the most famous ruling I ever received as a player, and certainly the one I remember most vividly, brought this rule into play.

It was the 1958 Masters. After rounds of 70, 73, and 68, and a solid front-nine performance on Sunday, I entered Amen Corner, the most famous stretch of holes in championship golf, with a one-stroke advantage. I was pumped. I'd never won a professional major, and I knew I was playing well enough to win this one. If I could negotiate the final seven holes at Augusta National, I would join players like Ben Hogan and Sam Snead as a Masters winner.

At the par-three 12th, the most treacherous short hole in tournament golf, I hit what I thought was a perfect shot, but I was more pumped than I realized and the ball flew over the green and into the fringe where it plugged in its own pitch mark.

At that time relief from an embedded ball was a local rule, not one of the rules of golf. That has since changed and Rule 25-2 deals with a ball that is embedded in its own pitch mark. In the spring of 1958 in Augusta there was no such rule. The ground was wet and sloppy, and a local rule providing relief for an embedded ball was in effect.

When I saw that my ball was embedded behind the 12th green, I called a rules official over and explained my situation, fully expecting him to give me the relief I was entitled to under the local rule. By all rights I should have been able to lift, clean, and drop my ball without penalty to a spot as close as possible to the original position and no nearer the hole. That's exactly the way we'd been playing all week.

So imagine my surprise when the rules official, a fellow named Arthur Lacey, said, "No, you don't do that at Augusta."

"I beg your pardon?" I said. "We're playing wet-weather rules."

"No, sir," he said. "You can't do that. You've got to play it as it lies."

That sent my heart rate and blood pressure up a notch or two. I knew I was right, but I wasn't in much of a position to argue. Finally I said, "I'm going to play two balls and appeal to the tournament committee." I knew I had that option under Rule 3-3a. This was a stroke play competition, and there was definitely a doubt as to the procedure, not on my part, but on the part of one of the officials.

"No, sir," Mr. Lacey said with a slight edge to his voice. "You cannot do that either."

That's when I knew my official was out of bounds. There was a one-in-a-million chance that I was wrong about the embedded ball rule. Even though it had been in effect all week, I could have been wrong. It could have been rescinded on Sunday without my knowledge. But I knew I was right about playing a second ball. That is always an option under the rules.

"Well," I said, "that's exactly what I'm doing."

In accordance with Rule 3-3a as I knew it, I played the ball, the embedded ball still buried in its pitchmark, and took a double-bogey. Then I returned to the spot where the original ball had been, and I dropped a second ball. From there I chipped up to about three feet and made that putt for par, much to the chagrin of Mr. Lacey, who stood stoically nearby.

The scoreboards around the course showed that I had made a double bogey on the 12th, dropping me from one ahead to being one behind. But I didn't let it rattle me. I knew I was right.

On the 13th, Bob Jones rode down on his golf cart and watched me. I hit the green on the par-five with a 3-wood and made a 20-foot putt for eagle. Then I parred 14. After my tee shot on 15, I was summoned over to the side of the fairway where a group of men in green jackets, including Bob Jones, were discussing my situation. When I arrived at the gathering the tournament committee chairman said, "Mr. Palmer, the committee has ruled in your favor. You will have a three at the twelfth hole."

All the scoreboards were changed to reflect my par at the 12th, which sent some confusion through the galleries, and some consternation through the ranks of my fellow competitors. It was still a tight squeeze. I bogeyed the 16th and the 18th for a 73–284, and a one-shot victory. I later heard that Ken Venturi was particularly upset, feeling like he had been cheated by my second-ball situation at the 12th. But I felt then and I feel now that I did what any other player could and should do: I followed the rules in both letter and spirit, and, as a result, I won my first major championship title.

It was only after playing a second ball and winning an appeal that I was able to capture the 1958 Masters tournament and wear my first Green Jacket.
ARNOLD PALMER'S PERSONAL COLLECTION

Clubs

and

Balls

In addition to governing the way in which we play the game, the USGA and the R&A also set rules for the types of clubs we can use. There's been a great deal of discussion and disagreement on this subject recently, and I've found myself in the middle of a gentlemanly disagreement with the USGA on certain technical rulings relating to clubs (a subject I go into in the Afterword of this book). But there are certain rules relating to clubs that have nothing to do with technical mind-numbing minutiae like "coefficient of restitution." Those rules are important to note, because the consequences for club-related rules mistakes can be devastating.

The part of Rule 4 where players sometimes get into trouble is the section concerning altering the characteristics of your golf clubs during a round. **Rule 4-2a** reads:

> **During a stipulated round, the playing charac-teristics of a club shall not be purposely changed by adjustment or by any other means.**

That means you can't bend the shaft of a club during a round to give the club more or less loft or a flatter or more upright lie. The clubs you start with are the clubs you play with throughout the round.

You also can't add any foreign material to a club. In the old days when woods were actually made of wood, it wasn't uncommon to see jars of Vaseline in some players' golf bags. When applied to the face of a wood, the substance would cut down on spin, ostensibly making drives go straighter. In addition to cheating, I always thought this was a stupid idea. Sure, your ball flies straighter off a wooden club coated with Vaseline, but if the shot starts off line, all you've done is hit it straighter into the trees.

Cheating aside, sometimes a club is unintentionally altered during a round. In those instances, the remedy relies a great deal on intent. According to Rule 4-3, if a club is damaged in the normal course of play, with no malicious or hostile intent or action on the part of the player, you can either continue to play with the damaged club if it conforms to the rules; repair the damaged club, or have it repaired as long as the process doesn't delay play;

or replace the damaged club with another club as long as the replacement club conforms to the Rules.

In the 1999 Tour Championship, Tiger Woods had just such an option at his disposal. On the par-four 15th hole on Thursday, Tiger drove his ball in the right rough, under a tree, and next to a rock. The rock was about twice the size of the golf ball, but the ball was touching it. "If I moved the rock, the ball would move," Tiger said. "I would have incurred a penalty [under Rule 18-2c]."

His other option was to take an unplayable lie, but his drop options weren't very good. "If I had taken two club lengths for an unplayable lie I would still have been in the rough with a tree in my line, and I probably wouldn't have saved par."

So Tiger took an unusual step. He hit the rock first, under the assumption that if he could advance the rock toward the fairway, the ball had a good chance of following. The only problem with that strategy was the fact that rocks are harder than golf balls. Tiger advanced the ball (although he didn't get it out of the rough) and ruined a golf club in the process.

"My club had a hole in the face," he said. "It squashed the club face so the grooves were completely flat. It was an incredible shot."

Even though Tiger consciously decided to take a swing at a rock instead of a ball, the resulting damage to his club, under the rules, was part of the "normal course of play." As a result, Tiger could have exercised his options under Rule 4-3. There was no way he could have repaired the club without delaying play, and he couldn't play the club with a hole in the face, so his only other option was to replace it, which he did.

Then there are those who damage their clubs through acts outside the normal course of play; little things like slamming clubs into the ground and breaking the shafts, or wrapping them around trees in fits of anger. I never personally had to consult the rule book for those kinds of situations, because I didn't throw my clubs or bang them around in anger. If I had done anything like that my Pap would have levied more severe justice on me than anything the USGA or R&A could have meted out. But there are plenty of guys who have had such troubles while playing golf, and a fair number who have run afoul of the rules in the process.

According to **Rule 4-3b**:

> **If, during a stipulated round, a player's club is damaged other than in the normal course of play rendering it non-conforming or changing its playing characteristics, the club shall not subsequently be used or replaced during the round.**

During the 1987 Ryder Cup Matches at Muirfield Village in Columbus, Ohio, Ben Crenshaw became so angry at his putting performance that he slammed his putter against his own foot, breaking the shaft of the club.

A temper tantrum doesn't fall within the guidelines of "normal course of play," so Crenshaw couldn't repair or replace his putter. He finished the match (which he lost) putting with a 1-iron. Afterward, Captain Jack Nicklaus turned to Crenshaw and said, "You broke what!"

It's an incident Crenshaw would rather forget, but a rule that everyone should remember.

Poor Dudley Hart has trouble containing his emotions, and that sometimes gets him into trouble. ASSOCIATED PRESS/AP

Dudley Hart didn't break his putter during the little tantrum he threw at the 2001 Bob Hope Chrysler Classic, but he probably wishes he had. After bending the putter in a manner "outside the normal course of play," as PGA Tour officials described it, Hart continued to putt with the putter. That's a no-no. The bent putter didn't have the same playing characteristics, so the club could no longer be used.

When informed of the situation, Hart admitted to the infraction and accepted the penalty of disqualification.

The other rule concerning clubs that has gotten a lot of attention recently is **Rule 4-4a**, which says, in part:

> **The player shall start a stipulated round with not more than fourteen clubs.**

You can start with fewer than fourteen clubs. You can even add clubs after you've started the round provided the maximum number of clubs in your bag never exceeds fourteen and you don't borrow a club from anyone else playing on the course, but you can never, ever have more than fourteen clubs in a competitive round of golf.

This rule stems from the 1936 Walker Cup matches, an amateur team competition between the United States and Great Britain and Ireland. Shortly after Lawson Little, one of the players on the winning America squad, was found to have thirty-two clubs in his bag, the R&A and USGA convened and set the number fourteen as the limit.

That brings us to the 2001 British Open Championship at Royal Lytham and St. Annes in Lancaster, northern England. Trailing by a single shot going into the final round, Ian Woosnam, playing his best golf in two years and trying to win the championship that means the most to him, stood on the tee at the par-three first, drew his 6-iron, and hit a perfect shot that rolled within two inches of the cup. The crowd erupted, and the battle was joined. Woosnam tapped in for a birdie, and marched to the second tee with a share of the lead.

Then things got ugly. Woosnam's caddie, Miles Byrne, could barely light his cigarette his hands were trembling so badly. The news he had to deliver to his boss was not good. "You're going to go ballistic," Byrne said, his Irish voice quivering.

"What is it?" Woosnam asked.

"We've got two drivers," Byrne told his boss. "That's fifteen."

Byrne was right on two fronts: They had fifteen clubs in the bag, and his boss did, indeed, go ballistic. Woosnam stormed around the tee, pulling his hat off, then throwing it back on his head in a slightly cockeyed manner. He threw the extra driver out of his bag, then yelled and stomped and swore some more. In the end, he turned to John Paramour, the rules official on the scene, and said, "How many, John?"

Paramour held up two fingers. That was it. Woosnam's first-hole birdie became a bogey. Rather than being tied for the lead, he was two shots back. Rather than building momentum, he spent the remainder of the round trying to forget what had happened.

"I did not really get it out of my head the whole way around," Woosnam said. "I kept thinking that if I hadn't had the penalty I

Ian Woosnam removes his 15th club during the 2001 British Open Championship. MICHAEL C. COHEN

could have been leading or the joint leader. I felt like picking up and walking in."

Woosnam had been doing what a lot of us do prior to a round, working with two different drivers while trying to decide which one held the magic formula for the day. He fiddled around a bit too long, though, arriving at the first tee just two minutes before his scheduled tee time.

"Normally, an R&A official would say something like 'Gentlemen, have you counted the clubs?'" said R&A official Hugh Campbell. "They usually look at you like you've lost your marbles. But this time we didn't have time to ask, because they arrived on the tee moments before going off."

Had the first hole been anything but a par-three, the error might have been caught, since reaching for a driver and finding two in the bag would give you a strong hint that something was awry. Regardless, Woosnam made no excuses. He took his medicine like a man. He clawed his way back to finish tied for third, leaving the links in Lytham with a faraway look in his eyes.

Woosnam's error wasn't the first time a player has mistakenly teed off with too many clubs in the bag. Johnny Miller played an entire round in the U.S. Open with one of his son's plastic clubs stuffed in the bottom of his bag. At the conclusion of the round Miller asked the rules official if the club was actually considered a club. "Let's see," the official said, "it has a head, a grip, and a shaft, so it's a golf club." The penalty for Miller was four shots, the maximum allowed under the rule.

Jack Nicklaus has made the mistake twice, once as a player and another time as a caddie. The first incident occurred in a team match in Canada in the 1960s when Jack was playing with Deane Beman. According to Jack, "We were on the fifth hole in an alternate shot contest when Deane and I discovered that Deane had two wedges in his bag. The penalty in match play was the loss of all five holes we had played. We were five down immediately because neither of us had checked the bag."

The other incident occurred in a U.S. Open qualifying round when Jack, caddying for his son Gary, inadvertently left his own 4-iron in Gary's bag. "On the third hole Gary wanted to hit a

Johnny Miller was penalized for having too many clubs after discovering one of his son's plastic drivers in the bottom of his bag. ASSOCIATED PRESS/AP

Even the best make mistakes. Jack Nicklaus, caddying for his son, Gary, failed to count the clubs in Gary's bag during U.S. Open qualifying. A 15th club cost Gary four penalty shots. ASSOCIATED PRESS/AP

four-iron," Jack said. "I looked in the bag and said, 'Do you want to play my four-iron or your four-iron?' I'd counted the clubs by number one, two, three, etcetera. But I didn't see that there were two four-irons in the bag."

Jack summed up his and Woosnam's mistake correctly, however, when he said, "I made the mistake, but ultimately, it's the player's responsibility."

Rule 5 dealing with balls is a lot easier, simply because it's so hard to screw it up. As long as you don't add any foreign substances to your ball, and you correctly mark and inform your fellow competitors before taking a damaged ball out of play, you're in pretty good shape on this one.

There could be times when you play in events in which the Committee may require you to play with balls on the USGA list of "Conforming Golf Balls." Greg Norman ran afoul of that rule by playing a prototype ball in a sanctioned event that hadn't been officially added to the USGA's list. Norman was disqualified, even though the ball later passed inspection.

Unless you're on a ball manufacturer's prototype list, or unless you buy your golf balls on the black market or through an 800 number, you're probably safe. But it's always a good idea to check the local rules before teeing off in any event. You never know what you might find.

Greg Norman learned a hard lesson about conforming and nonconforming equipment when he played a ball that had nonapproved markings. ASSOCIATED PRESS/AP

The Player

Golf is a game in which the player is ultimately responsible for all of his and his caddie's actions. That's what makes golf so different from other sports. Rather than having officials standing by to enforce the rules, golfers are responsible for knowing the rules and playing by them at all times. A player must know what the format of the competition is, and when to be on the first tee. Those obligations are inviolable.

In the 1940 U.S. Open, Porky Oliver shot a final round 71 and thought he was in a playoff with Lawson Little and Gene Sarazen. Instead Porky was disqualified for having started his final round before his scheduled tee time. A storm was brewing, and Porky, along with five other players, wanted to get their rounds in, so, while Joe Dey, the official starter, was in the clubhouse eating lunch, three groups teed off in violation of **Rule 6- 3a** that states:

The player shall start at the time laid down by the Committee.

Porky started early, and paid a hefty price for his error. When informed afterward that instead of being in the playoff he was disqualified, Porky sat in the locker room and wept. Both Little and Sarazen appealed to the USGA to allow Porky to play, but the Committee wouldn't budge. Penalty for breach of Rule 6-3a was disqualification, and that's the penalty Porky received.

As tough as that story seems, it's not the harshest ruling ever levied under Rule 6. There is another recent ruling that makes Porky's lost U.S. Open appear mild.

It occurred on Father's Day in the year 2000, the same day Tiger Woods was setting a new U.S. Open record at Pebble Beach. But one state east of the Monterey Peninsula, a terrible situation was brewing in the Arizona Mid-Amateur championship. Through 45 holes of the tournament being played at the Ocotillo Golf Club in Chandler, forty-three-year-old Lieutenant Colonel Mark Johnson held a commanding 11-shot lead, and appeared to be on his way to certain victory. To help celebrate the moment, Colonel Johnson invited his son, Seth, who was celebrating his fourteenth birthday, to caddie for him, even though Seth walked slowly and had a lazy eye that made it difficult to judge depth perception. The colonel had carried his own bag during the first two rounds, but what the heck? It was his son's birthday, and Father's Day to boot.

Porky Oliver beat the rain but lost his best shot at the U.S. Open title after teeing off before his prescribed time. ASSOCIATED PRESS/ AP

At the turn, they stopped to talk to Robert (Doc) Graves, who imparted the bad news. Colonel Johnson was disqualified.

The infraction occurred back on the third hole, when Seth, who had invited a twelve-year-old friend, Derek Harris, pulled the putter out of the bag and allowed Derek to carry it down the third fairway. Derek waggled the putter the way any twelve-year-old would. Then Derek handed it to Colonel Johnson.

Graves saw the whole thing. Within minutes he was on his walkie-talkie, discussing the issue with the Committee.

The Committee subsequently ruled that Johnson had employed two caddies, a violation of **Rule 6-4**, which reads in part:

> **The player may have only one caddie at any one time, under penalty of disqualification.**

They told Colonel Johnson, his fourteen-year-old caddie, and the caddie's twelve-year-old friend to go home, which is exactly what the Colonel did, helping the sobbing boys into his pickup truck and driving two and a half hours back to Sierra Vista. They opened Seth's birthday presents that night, and Colonel Johnson opened his Father's Day gift, but nobody in the family celebrated.

Back in Chandler, Arizona Golf Association officials were saying things like, "The rules of golf are like the honor code the military academies have, and we are here to apply the rules." Chandler called it, "The toughest call I've had to make in twenty-five years," but he went on to say, "We had to protect the field."

Protecting the field from a twelve-year-old didn't fly very far in the golf community. Within a week of the ruling the Arizona Golf Association couldn't have been more unpopular if they had joined the Manson family. The ruling was all the buzz on the PGA and Senior PGA Tours in the days that followed. Even Peter Dawson, the secretary of the R&A, shook his head and said, "Unbelievable," when he heard about the ruling.

My friend Curtis Strange wrote an opinion piece that called the officials "overzealous." Curtis went on to say, "The Rules are in place to protect each player and his fellow competitors, but they also have to be fair. Intent must be judged, as well as the spirit of the game. One of the basics of the game is that it is introduced from parents to children. It would be tragic if the boys were pushed away from golf because of one overzealous rules official."

I agree with Curtis. The AGA had an out. They could have deemed Derek's action "a casual act of someone assisting a player," which is what you have when a gallery member retrieves your hat that has blown off, or a second caddie retrieves the wedge you accidentally left beside the sand trap. There's a decision on Rule 6-4 that deals with just such occurrences, and the result is "no penalty."

The Arizona Golf Association missed one, big time, when they disqualified Colonel Johnson. And it is the Committee, not the man they disqualified, who must live with the backlash from their decision.

Another near-miss regarding **Rule 6-6** occurred in Tampa, Florida. That rule states:

6-6a After each hole the marker should check the score with the competitor and record it. On completion of the round the marker shall sign the card and hand it to the competitor. If more than one marker records the scores, each shall sign for the part for which he is responsible.

6-6b After completion of the round, the competitor should check his score for each hole and settle any doubtful points with the Committee. He shall ensure that the marker has signed the card, countersign the card himself and return it to the Committee as soon as possible.

Excerpt from **Rule 6-6d:**

The competitor is responsible for the correctness of the score recorded for each hole on his card.

Matthew Ross, a nine-year-old with autism, loves the game and plays quite well. He has won several Special Olympic events, and defeated other children in competition who suffer no developmental difficulties. His first word was "bogey," and his physical, psychological, and social development has progressed at an accelerated rate for an autistic child because of his exposure to golf.

But Matthew can't keep his own score, or the score of a fellow competitor. He can hit the shots. He can walk the course. He can carry his own bag, and hole all his putts like the other kids, but his mental facilities are not such that he can keep track of scores. For a Tampa Junior Golf Association, that was fine for an eight-year-old, but, initially they ruled that once Matthew or any other player turned nine, they had to keep their own scores. In a written statement, TJGA president Brian Code said Matthew's participation would "be unfair to the other competitors."

Matthew's mother got a lawyer, and the TJGA was bombarded by letters of outrage from parents. Even the USGA got involved, sending a letter to the TJGA saying they could, indeed, write a local rule allowing Matthew to have a scorer.

I certainly believe that, as a private organization, the Tampa Junior Golf Association has the right to make its own rules, and I would fight for them to be able to hold on to that right. But they initially missed the boat with this one. Fortunately common sense prevailed, and the TJGA amended its rules to allow Matthew to have a "mentor" who would perform no caddie functions, but who could keep the child's score. Everyone agreed that if Matthew broke any rules resulting in disqualification he would, indeed, be disqualified, but he could continue to play out his round. It would be up to his mother to decide whether to break the news to her son about his disqualification.

I'm happy that this situation was resolved before lawyers and judges got hold of it. Our game is about honor and integrity, but it's also about common sense. I'm glad the TJGA realized the error of its ways and allowed Matthew Ross to play.

While we're on the subject of keeping score, one of the most famous rules incidents in the history of golf centered on the last section of **Rule 6-6**, which reads:

> **If he returns a score for any hole lower than actually taken, he shall be disqualified. If he returns a score for any hole higher than actually taken, the score as returned shall stand.**

At Augusta National in 1968, that rule came to the attention of the golfing world. It was the final round of the Masters, and Argentina's Roberto de Vicenzo was making a charge. De Vicenzo shot 31 on the front nine on Sunday to claw his way into the hunt. Then he birdied the par-three 12th, and the par-five 15th to gain a share of the lead. Another birdie at the 17th gave de Vicenzo the lead outright with one hole to play. When he made a bogey at the 18th, it appeared that de Vicenzo was on his way to a playoff with Bob Goalby the following day.

Then the most famous scoring error in golf occurred. De Vicenzo, along with his playing partner and scorer, Tommy Aaron, sat down at the small scorers' table set up behind the 18th green at Augusta National. It was an odd scoring setup for a tournament that was so magnificently run in every other respect—a one-man operation with no privacy from the galleries and no one there to double-check the scores. Joe Dey, by then the executive director of the USGA, had warned Clifford Roberts, the Masters tournament chairman, about the dangers of the setup and

Calling himself "a stupid," Roberto de Vicenzo's expression tells the story after signing an incorrect scorecard at the 1968 Masters. ASSOCIATED PRESS/AP

what could possibly happen, but the Masters kept the scoring table through 1968.

De Vicenzo, an affable guy and a great player, chatted with the official on the scene, and with Goalby and his playing partner, Raymond Floyd, who were nearby. In all his chatting and waving to the crowd, de Vicenzo mistakenly signed an incorrect scorecard. Aaron had given de Vicenzo a four on the 17th instead of the birdie three he had made. De Vicenzo hadn't caught the mistake, and he signed for a score higher than the one actually made.

The rule was clear: The higher score stood and Bob Goalby won the 1968 Masters.

De Vicenzo slumped in the chair and put his head in his hands muttering, "What a stupid I am," over and over again. It was a painful moment to watch, and a part of golf history that no one will ever forget.

Roberto wasn't the first professional to suffer a loss because of an error on his scorecard. In 1966 Doug Sanders led the Pensacola Open after two rounds, but while Doug was talking to the media after his round, Jack Tuthill, a PGA Tour rules official at the time, informed Doug that he hadn't signed his scorecard on Friday. Because play had started on both one and ten in Pensacola, Doug had finished his round on the ninth hole, a good hike from the scorer's tent. Doug being Doug, he signed autographs and flirted with all the girls around the clubhouse, but never got around to signing his card. As a result Tuthill was faced with no choice but to disqualify him. Doug was furious at the time, but he learned a valuable lesson. From that moment on, I never saw him speak to a soul after a round until he had checked and signed his scorecard.

Not quite as famous as de Vicenzo, but certainly as expensive a gaffe came in the 2000 Benson and Hedges International Open. Leading by five shots through three rounds, Ireland's Padraig

Harrington looked unbeatable. He was playing some of the best golf of his life, so well in fact that the Belfry Hotel, where the tournament was played, asked officials if they could have copies of Harrington's scorecards for framing. Such items are usually hung in the club, given to the player, or auctioned off for charity. It's a pretty common practice on all tours.

What wasn't common was what the tournament officials found. According to European Tour senior referee Andy McFee, "In the process of gathering the cards, our staff noticed that while his first-round card had two signatures on it, neither was Padraig's. Nowhere is there an attestation from the player that the round is accurate. That is a breach of the rules. The penalty is disqualification."

Thirty minutes before Harrington was set to tee off in a tournament with victory seemingly at hand, he was informed that he wouldn't be playing. "I saw two signatures on the card, and didn't pay attention to the fact that neither one was mine," Harrington said. "It was stupid."

But as McFee said, it was also part of the game. "This goes to the very core of golf," he said. "Golf is not played in the constant gaze of a referee, and because of that it is easy to do things that are not correct. At the end of the day you have to hold up your card to the rest of the world. It's a core principle. Still, I wish to hell it hadn't happened."

So do Harrington, de Vicenzo, and the thousands of other golfers throughout the world who have erred in exactly the same way.

Practice

I love to practice. Even at my age, I'm still learning new things about the game and I am constantly itching to get on the practice tee and try out this new move or that new technique. Even on the golf course, when I'm playing alone or in a leisurely round with some friends, I'll throw a couple of balls down and practice various shots with different clubs. It's a big part of what makes the game fun.

In a tournament, however, I rarely ever hit a practice putt, in part because I've never felt comfortable delaying play by taking extra putts after the hole has been completed, and in part because any other form of practice is against the rules.

Rule 7 deals with practice, when and how a player can practice, and under what conditions practice can occur on the course. This is one of the rules in which what you can do in match play and what you can do in stroke play are vastly different. **Rule 7-1a** reads:

> **On any day of a match play competition, a player may practice on the competition course before a round.**

But the rule is completely different for a stroke play competition. There, **Rule 7-1b** reads:

> **On any day of a stroke competition or play-off, a competitor shall not practice on the competition course or test the surface of any putting green on the course before a round or play-off. When two or more rounds of a stroke competition are to be played over consecutive days, a competitor shall not practice between those rounds on any competition course remaining to be played, or test the surface of any putting green on such course.**

One of the more popular figures, even with the American crowds, at the 1999 Ryder Cup matches in Massachusetts was the Frenchman Jean Van de Velde. Less than 100 days after his spectacular collapse in the British Open at Carnoustie, Scotland, where Van de Velde came to the 72nd hole leading by three shots and took a triple-bogey seven to fall into a playoff and lose, the handsome Van de Velde made his Ryder Cup debut at the Country Club in Brookline. The crowds loved him, in part because he had

Jean Van de Velde had plenty of practice rounds under his belt before tee-ing off on Sunday in the 1999 Ryder Cup matches. MICHAEL C. COHEN

handled himself with such dignity after his loss in Scotland, and in part because all the fans could relate to him. Everyone who has ever played golf has had brain lock at some point, and everyone (or so it seemed) who had ever blown a three-shot lead in a two-dollar nassau was in Brookline cheering for Van de Velde.

There was only one problem: Van de Velde didn't play a single match until Sunday when he went out in a match against Davis Love III. But that didn't stop Van de Velde from practicing, nor did it stop the galleries in Brookline from cheering his every move. After the fourball and foursome matches went out on Friday and Saturday, Van de Velde was behind them, hitting practice shots to the greens and taking his time learning the intricacies of the golf course.

He could do that because the Ryder Cup is a match play contest, and Rule 7 allowed it. Had it been a stroke play competition, Van de Velde's practice would have been relegated to the driving range and putting green after the first tee shot of competition was struck. But because of the rule regarding practice, Van de Velde, and the other players from both sides who were not involved in the day's competition, could practice on the golf course behind the matches being contested.

Bob Murphy, however, couldn't practice putt in the 12th fairway during the first round of the 1995 Burnet Senior Classic, but that's exactly what Murph did. After two weather delays, Murph returned to the 12th hole and awaited the horn to blow signaling the resumption of play.

Murph's practice habits got him into a world of trouble on the Senior PGA Tour. ASSOCIATED PRESS/AP

While waiting, Murph strolled the area around his ball mark, chatting with his caddie and his playing partners. He took a few practice swings, and meandered back and forth. Then he threw down a ball—the very ball he was about to put into play once play resumed—and he knocked a few shots around with his putter.

You could hardly call it "practice" in a literal sense of the word. Murph had hit shots with a putter on the fairway. He was neither testing his stroke nor gauging the speed of the fairways. He was killing time.

He was also killing his chances at a victory. Mike Joyce noticed Murphy's action, and wondered at the time if it was legal. But Joyce didn't say anything that Friday, nor did he say anything on Saturday after Murph shot a second consecutive 69. It wasn't until Sunday morning in the locker room that Joyce brought the incident to Murph's attention.

Murph immediately consulted with tour officials, who informed him that he had, indeed, broken Rule 7. Because the incident had occurred on Friday, and Murph had failed to assess himself the two-shot penalty such an infraction required, he had technically signed an incorrect scorecard. Minutes later Murph was cleaning out his locker and heading home. He was disqualified.

Had he fired a third round of 69, Murph would have finished fifth and won $40,000. As it was, he went home having learned a valuable lesson about how not to while away his idle time.

Advice;
Indicating Line of Play

The rule prohibiting advice is a tough one for golfers to obey because most golfers are genuinely helpful people. If a fellow competitor is struggling, we want to help by offering a tidbit of counsel or encouragement, something like "You're moving your head on your putts," or "You need to take one more club here because the hole plays longer than it looks." This is the nature of golf and golfers. We're nice people.

The problem is, in competition, such advice is illegal under **Rule 8-1**, which reads:

> **During a stipulated round, a player shall not give advice to anyone in the competition except his partner and may ask for advice only from his partner or either of their caddies.**

The question then becomes, what is advice? Can you tell someone that a creek runs across the fairway if you can't see it from
the tee? Can you tell someone how deep a pin is cut on the
green, or that there's a hidden pot bunker on the far side of yon-
der knoll? If you can't give a lesson, can you say, "Hey, your tim-
ing's a little off today. Maybe you should take one more club and
swing a little slower," or is that against the rules? What consti-
tutes advice and what is considered normal conversation
between friendly golfers?

Rule 8 attempts to explain the difference, giving a definition
of advice that reads as follows:

> **"Advice" is any counsel or suggestion which could
> influence a player in determining his play, the
> choice of a club or the method of making a stroke.
> Information on the Rules or on matters of pub-
> lic information, such as the position of hazards
> or the flagstick on the putting green, is not advice.**

If the information is public knowledge, it can be shared. If it's
something you've noticed about your opponent's swing, or if it
relates to what club a player should use on a particular hole, or
which shot might be most appropriate under certain conditions,
that's considered "advice" and is prohibited. You can't give it, and
you can't ask for it.

You can go out of your way to make public declarations to
the gallery, your caddie, or anyone else who will listen—things

like "Boy, that was a solid six-iron," or "Man, I didn't realize the air was so thick. The ball isn't carrying as far today as I thought it would"—and even though your fellow competitor hears these things and can put them to use, it isn't considered advice. It's when you say to another competitor, "I hit a six-iron," or "Did you hit a six-iron?" that you run afoul of the rules.

Even when you say it in the heat of the moment with the intent of doing everything but help, it's still considered advice. Consider the plight of Greg Chalmers. At the opening round of the Kemper Open, Chalmers was growing annoyed with his fellow competitor's caddie. The caddie kept peeking into Chalmers's bag to see what club he was hitting, a practice that is perfectly legal since the caddie was neither asking for nor receiving "advice." After hitting one poor shot, Chalmers turned to find the offending caddie back at his bag. "I hit a six-iron, okay," Chalmers snapped. "Now, just get away from me."

Nobody said anything, and the caddie in question sulked off to the other side of the fairway. Thursday, Friday, and Saturday passed before Chalmers began thinking about what had happened. He was watching the Golf Channel when he heard about a similar incident on the Buy.com Tour that had resulted in a two-shot penalty under Rule 8. On Sunday morning, Chalmers approached Mark Russell, the PGA Tour official, with a question.

"Is it a violation?" Chalmers asked.

Russell was forced to break the bad news. Not only was it a violation that should have resulted in a two-shot penalty, Chalmers had signed an incorrect scorecard because he hadn't added the two shots to Thursday's round. He had to disqualify himself for signing an incorrect card. At the time he was tied for ninth, which

Greg Chalmers didn't mean to give advice when scolding a spying caddie, but his words cost him two shots. ASSOCIATED PRESS/CP

would have earned Chalmers around $95,000, but adhering to the rules was more important than the money.

"It just goes to show you what a gentleman's game golf is," Russell said. "If you're called out at first base, do you think the first baseman is going to say, 'Safe'?"

Raymond Floyd's wife, Maria, thought she saw the advice rule broken in the 1993 Ryder Cup when Seve Ballesteros pulled Jose Maria Olazabal aside during a match and started speaking in Spanish. Seve was quite animated in whatever he was saying to Olazabal, but Maria wasn't sure what the discussion was about since she didn't speak Spanish. "Can he do that?" she asked. Seve was a spectator and not Olazabal's partner in the match.

The answer depends on what was said. If Seve was cheering Olazabal on, saying something like, "Go get 'em, big guy. You can do it," then there was no violation. If, however, he said something like "You've got to hit one more club than normal on all these par-threes. They're all playing long today," or "You're moving your head on your wedge shots and hitting them fat," then that would be a violation of Rule 8. But since Maria has no idea what was said, it's impossible to know.

Information
as to Strokes Taken

This one is simple: You count all strokes including penalty strokes, and you inform your fellow competitors, scorers, markers, officials, etcetera, when you've incurred a penalty stroke. If you see your opponent in match play break a rule, you call it right then and there. You can't save up your penalties and pull a "gotcha" later in the match.

That's it. That's all Rule 9 says. But the implications for golfers are more far-reaching than that.

Just as Greg Chalmers had to clear his conscience about inadvertently giving advice in an earlier round (see Rule 8) golfers are constantly calling penalties on themselves, even when no one else is watching.

One of the most chronicled incidents of a player's honesty and integrity involved the great amateur Bob Jones, the only player in history to win the British Amateur, British Open, U.S.

Amateur, and U.S. Open titles in the same year. At the time those four events constituted the Grand Slam of Golf, and in 1930 when Jones completed the feat at Merion Golf Club in Philadelphia, it was a sporting accomplishment unlike anything the world had ever seen.

But five years earlier, Jones had established a benchmark for honor and integrity in the game. It was the 1925 U.S. Open at Worcester Country Club in Worcester, Massachusetts, an event that became more of a marathon than a golf tournament. Temperatures swelled above 100 degrees every day, and before the conclusion of play Jones had lost twelve pounds. He had also lost the tournament by a single shot in a 36-hole playoff to Willie MacFarlane.

As is the case in any major golf tournament, past or present, pundits replayed every shot, trying to find the shot of the tournament or the turning point that made the difference. In this case it wasn't hard to find. Jones had called a penalty on himself in the opening round.

It occurred on the 11th hole when Jones hooked his tee shot into high grass left of the fairway. As he addressed the ball in the rough, Jones thought he saw the ball move. No one else could see the ball, much less see whether or not it had changed locations on the ground. But Jones didn't hesitate. He informed his marker that the ball had moved and he assessed himself a one-shot penalty.

When he was later praised for the action, Jones became annoyed, saying, "You might as well praise a man for not robbing a bank."

After the incident O. B. Keeler, the great chronicler of Jones's life and career, summed up that Open and the impact it had on

Perhaps the most famous penalty in golf at the time was the one-shot Bob
Jones called on himself when his ball moved in the 1925 U.S. Open.
ASSOCIATED PRESS

the game. Keeler wrote, "There are things in golf finer than winning championships."

Countless other golfers have called penalties on themselves in
the almost eighty years since Jones lost that U.S. Open. It's a staple of our sport that no amount of money can change.

Even caddies understand the code of honor that binds golfers
together. At the 2001 Welch's/Circle K Championship, Tom Hanson, a caddie for Sue Ginter, witnessed an incident in the third
round that made his heart sink. On the par-four second hole Ginter was in a large bunker. When her swing failed to advance the

ball out of the bunker, she let her frustrations overwhelm her and she banged her club into the sand. Ginter didn't realize that her actions constituted a penalty. Hanson did.

"I immediately realized she had done something irreversible," he said. "According to the rules of golf, Sue shouldn't have grounded her club in the bunker with her ball still in the hazard, even though her ball was some twenty yards away. I quickly looked around to see if anyone else had seen the infraction. Unfortunately for me, our playing partner, Sherri Steinhauer, was on the green preparing to putt for birdie and didn't get a good view, and the fans following us were few and far between. The only witness was me."

Hanson wrestled with his conscience, but only briefly. He knew what his boss would want. So after Ginter successfully got up and down for what appeared to be a bogey, he broke the news.

"I informed her of the penalty, and she quickly realized I was right," Hanson said. "She turned to Steinhauer and took her punishment—a two-shot penalty—like a champion."

Order of Play

The rules on who plays first, second, third, and so on are spelled out in unambiguous detail in Rule 10. To summarize the rule, the side with the honor on the first hole—that is, the side that gets to tee off first—is determined by blind draw. This is a little like flipping a coin to start a football game. The side that wins the draw gets to hit first off the first tee. After that, the side (or competitor) that has the lowest score on the hole wins the honor on the next tee.

In the fairway, rough, or hazards between the tee and the cup, the player who is farthest from the hole plays first. If you can't decide who's farther away, you flip a coin, draw straws, pick a number, or come up with some other "lot" determination for the order of play.

The honor and the order of play in a stroke play competition isn't a huge consideration, primarily because there's no penalty for playing out of turn. If a player trots off to the rest room between holes, it's common for his fellow competitors to go ahead and tee off rather than delay play by waiting for the player with the honor to conduct his personal business. The same is true in the fairway. If there is a delay of some sort, it's common for the player who is away to say, "Go ahead if you're ready," thus giving up the right to play first to another player. This happens all the time.

When it becomes illegal is when players on the first tee agree to waive the honor rule. It's common in friendly games for players to say, "Okay, guys, we don't have a lot of time today, so let's play 'ready golf.' When you're ready hit it, and don't worry about the honor." If anything, this kind of arrangement speeds up play. But it's also a violation of part of Rule 1: Agreement to Waive Rules Prohibited.

If you agree to waive this rule to aid a particular competitor in stroke play, the Committee can deem you to have violated this rule and disqualify you as well. If, for example, in a stroke play competition you say, "Here, let me putt first even though you're away so I can show you the line and speed of the putt," you've given one competitor—the one watching your putt—an advantage over the rest of the field. That's a penalty that can, and should, result in disqualification. Other playing-out-of-turn infractions in stroke play might be considered rude, but they aren't punishable with any sort of penalty.

Match play is a different story. In a match if you play out of turn, **Rule 10-1c** reads as follows:

> **If a player plays when his opponent should have played, the opponent may immediately require the**

player to cancel the stroke so played and, in correct order, play a ball without penalty as nearly as possible at the spot from which the original ball was last played (see Rule 20-5).

This rule was put to the test in a somewhat controversial way during the 2000 Solheim Cup at Loch Lomond in Scotland. The Solheim Cup is the ladies' version of the Ryder Cup, in which teams from the United States and Europe meet biannually to play a series of matches for a cup named after Karsten Solheim, the founder and creator of Ping golf clubs. No money changes hands during the matches—there's no purse—and the Americans and Europeans slug it out for pride, honor, country, and goodwill in the name of golf.

But, according to the Europeans, there wasn't a lot of goodwill at the 2000 matches, especially after the last of the fourball matches.

The incident occurred early on Sunday, after rain had pushed what should have been Saturday afternoon matches into Sunday morning. On the 13th hole, with the United States team trailing Europe by the widest margin since these matches were first played in 1990, Kelly Robbins and Pat Hurst were trying desperately to eat into Europe's lead by defeating Annika Sorenstam and Janice Moodie in the fourball (or best ball) competition. The Americans were one-up through 12, and that lead looked good when both Moodie and Sorenstam missed the 13th green. Robbins had a lengthy birdie putt, but it appeared that the worst that would happen was a tie.

Then Sorenstam, from the front of the green, chipped in for birdie. The Swede danced on the edge of the green and celebrated with Moodie as the momentum seemed to shift in Europe's favor. But there was a problem. When Robbins, dejected by the chip-in, walked across the green to line up her putt, she saw that Sorenstam's ball had been four feet closer to the hole than her own ball. Sorenstam had played out of turn.

Referee Barb Trammell was called over to examine the situation. After pacing off the two spots, Trammell concluded that Sorenstam had, indeed, played out of turn. That prompted a call to chief referee Ian Randell, who outlined the Americans' options under Rule 10-1c. Robbins and Hurst could either let the chip-in stand, or order Sorenstam to replay the shot.

American team captain Pat Bradley, who had been involved in more than her share of controversies already, stepped in and took the decision away from Robbins and Hurst. Bradley had raised a few eyebrows shortly after her selection as captain when she grabbed Dale Eggeling's caddie by the shirt collar and shook him while screaming that the caddie had coughed during her backswing, an accusation the caddie denied. She was later criticized for her captain's picks—Brandie Burton and Beth Daniel—who happened to be pals of Bradley. But those decisions paled compared to Bradley's call that morning on the 13th green. Bradley never hesitated. Sorenstam would have to replay the chip.

The Swede was in tears. "I couldn't believe what she was saying, because I had already holed my chip," Sorenstam said. "I chipped and it went in and we were jumping up and down and cheering. I thought she was kidding. We all assumed it was my turn to chip, and both Kelly and Pat said, 'We assumed it was you.' Kelly had no intention of putting. She was standing with her hands folded watching my chip."

Intentions aren't a factor in Rule 10-1c, but it is one of the few rules in which a competitor is given an option to negate the shot of his or her competitor and force a replay. That's exactly what Bradley did, much to the chagrin of the Europeans.

"It makes you ask the question, what would they have done if I hadn't made it?" Sorenstam later lamented. "Who knows what the turn-out of the match would have been. The more I think about it the more mad I am. I can't believe they would call it after the fact. That's what gets me the most."

Sorenstam didn't make the chip the next time around, and Robbins and Hurst ended up winning the match 2-1. It didn't do much good. Later that day, Sweden's Carin Koch made a 15-foot birdie putt in the singles matches to clinch a victory for Europe. The controversial replay hadn't mattered in the overall outcome of the matches. All it did was fuel the acrimony between the two sides.

Bradley later said, "We played within the rules of the game. When the rules of golf are upheld, the spirit of the game is upheld."

I couldn't agree more, and I think all the whining about poor sportsmanship was ill timed and not very thoughtful. Sure, golf is a genteel game, but it's also competition. If you're playing this game at the highest level, you'd better be doing everything you can within the letter and spirit of the rules to beat your competitor, because your competitor is certainly going to try to beat you. Sorenstam was quick to condemn the Americans for making her replay the shot, but the truth of the matter was, it was

Sorenstam's fault for playing out of turn. If there was any question, she should have waited or measured. Bradley was well within her rights to force Sorenstam to replay that shot, and if the situation had been reversed, the European team could have (and should have) done the same thing.

The rule couldn't be clearer on the subject.

Pat Bradley took a lot of criticism for making Annika Sorenstam replay a shot in the 2000 Solheim Cup, but Bradley was well within her rights to do so. WARREN LITTLE/ALL SPORT

Teeing Ground

This is one of the most rudimentary rules in the book, and one of the most often misunderstood. Rule 11 deals with the teeing ground and what you can and can't do while on the tee. Most people know that you can't play from any spot forward of the tee markers, but a lot of people don't know that you can play from any spot within two club lengths behind the markers. The "teeing ground" as defined in the Rules, is:

> . . . the starting place for the hole to be played. It is a rectangular area two club-lengths in depth, the front and the sides of which are defined by the outside limits of two tee-markers. A ball is outside the teeing ground when all of it lies outside the teeing ground.

The player can certainly stand outside the tee markers to swing, as long as the ball (or a portion of the ball) is within the boundaries of that rectangle. But just because you can stand outside the markers doesn't mean the Committee must give you the entire area. At Pebble Beach, I've played the 18th many times when teeing the ball just inside the left-hand tee marker would require you to stand on the bank leading down to the Pacific Ocean. You could do that I guess, but why would you want to? It's not a requirement of the Committee or the grounds crew to afford you the entire teeing area. You certainly have the right to use it if you want, but that doesn't mean others have to bow to your wishes.

Most major tournament committees go out of their way to set the tees so that the entire teeing ground is available. When Phil Mickelson played in the 1998 Masters, he arrived at the newly built second tee on Thursday and immediately realized he had a problem. Phil wanted to tee up on the far right side of the tee. For most players that wouldn't be a problem. But because Phil plays left-handed, teeing on the right required that he stand outside the tee markers, exactly where the Augusta National Greens Committee had placed the water cooler.

Phil and his caddie solved the problem by moving the water cooler a few feet to the right. On the second green Phil's caddie, Jim (Bones) McKay, approached a man in a green jacket (one of Augusta's members) and said, "Hey, you guys didn't set up your water coolers with a left-handed player in mind. It's no big deal, but we just had to move the cooler on two tee."

It might not have been a big deal to Phil and Bones, but the members at Augusta thought differently. Before the day was over,

Phil Mickelson has always played well at the Masters, even when he's had to move a few things out of his way. MICHAEL C. COHEN

the Greens Committee chairman and several workers examined every tee box to ensure that such a situation never happened again. On Friday morning, as Bones was out checking pin placements before the second round, a maintenance worker approached him and said, "Man, I'm sorry about that cooler yesterday. We had a big meeting and got it taken care of."

"That's why this is the best golf tournament in the world," Phil said later. "Nothing slips through the cracks."

The other important portion of Rule 11 deals with a ball falling off a tee. Everybody has had a ball fall off the tee during address, a situation that usually prompts some comment from your partners like "There's one," or "At least it was straight." While not the least bit witty after all these years, those comments are also inaccurate. In plain English, **Rule 11-3** reads:

> **If a ball, when not in play, falls off a tee or is knocked off a tee by the player in addressing it, it may be re-teed without penalty, but if a stroke is made at the ball in these circumstances, whether the ball is moving or not, the stroke counts but no penalty is incurred.**

So if the ball is falling off the tee, either stop your swing or make a darn good one.

Searching for and Identifying the Ball

This is the first of four rules that deal with playing the ball, and it's about as straightforward as any rule in the rule book. To sum up the gist of the rule, a player is responsible for finding and identifying his own ball, no matter where it is or how it got there. If the ball is in a tree, and a hundred spectators saw it go into the tree, but neither the player nor the caddie can positively identify the ball, then the ball is lost, even though everyone knows it went into the tree.

Such was the situation for Japan's Tommy Nakajima at the 1987 U.S. Open at the Olympic Club in San Francisco. Nakajima was probably Japan's best player at the time, and he was certainly in contention in California. With strong support from a large number of Japanese citizens in the gallery, Nakajima was only two shots off the lead through 53 holes, and was looking to play in the penultimate group on Sunday when tragedy struck.

At only 347 yards, the finishing hole at Olympic isn't considered a "classic" closing hole, especially for a major championship. The green is small and severely sloped from back to front, which causes some strange things to happen, like balls rolling back down to the players' feet after putts have failed to crest the hill. But it was the tee shot that created problems for Nakajima.

Choosing to go with a driver, an aggressive play under tough U.S. Open conditions, Nakajima pushed his tee shot into the right rough. But it never hit the rough. The ball hit a tree—everybody saw it, even the TV cameras—but it never came down. The 18th green might not have been holding that day, but the tree certainly was. Nakajima's ball stuck in the top of the offending arbor and he couldn't find and identify it. Even when a fan, eighteen-year-old Kevin Moriarty, shimmied some forty feet up the tree trunk, the ball still couldn't be found and identified. Tommy, on the advice of rules official John Staver, declared the ball unplayable before Moriarty made his little climb, lest the ball be jilted free and a penalty incurred, but that turned out to be a moot point. The fact that everyone knew where the ball was didn't matter. Nakajima couldn't find it and identify it, so it was deemed to be lost.

He took double bogey on the final hole on Saturday and never recovered. After the round, Nakajima, who spoke only broken English, summed up the situation with one simple declaration: "That's golf," he said. Indeed, it is.

I had a similar experience in 1964 in the second round of the Australian Wills Masters tournament in Melbourne. After hook-

Tommy Nakajima's ball went into a tree on the 18th at Olympic and never came out. After taking a lost ball penalty, Nakajima uttered the words for which he is now famous: "That's golf." ASSOCIATED PRESS/AP

ing my tee shot on the ninth hole, I was told by the gallery members that my ball had lodged in the crook of a gum tree. Sure enough, I could see a ball in the fork of the tree, but from ground level, I couldn't identify it as mine. So I climbed the tree, carefully making my way up some twenty feet while being careful not to dislodge the ball and suffer a penalty stroke.

Once I got to it, I made the perfunctory identification. Then I decided that since I'd never climbed a tree in a round of golf before, I might as well take advantage of the situation. The ball was sitting nicely on the bark of the tree, and I had a nice solid perch from which to take a stance, so I decided to play it.

My caddie handed me a 1-iron and I turned it over so that the toe of the club was leading. With a hammer stroke, I chopped the ball out of the tree some thirty yards down the fairway. After extricating myself from the tree, I hit a great chip and rolled in about a 10-footer to save my par, proving once again that golf can be full of pleasant surprises. Anytime I'm asked what club I hit in that incident, however, I say "a tree-iron."

A ball in a tree isn't an everyday occurrence in golf, but it's not terribly unusual either. Still, some players get it wrong. At the Players Championship in 1999, Nick Faldo was disqualified after receiving some bad advice from his playing partner, Cory Pavin. The two were playing together at the TPC Sawgrass in Ponte Vedra, Florida, when Faldo stuck his ball in a palmetto tree. Both Faldo and Pavin could see the ball, but there was no way they could retrieve it.

Pavin told Faldo he had seen a similar incident in almost exactly the same spot a few years back involving Jose Maria Olazabal, and that Olazabal had simply taken an unplayable lie, and

Nick Faldo thought he could take a drop after his ball lodged in a tree at the 1999 Players Championship. He was wrong. ASSOCIATED PRESS/AP

dropped another ball accordingly. As it turned out Pavin had his facts right, but the ruling Olazabal had received turned out to be erroneous. So when Faldo took a similar drop without identifying his ball, he was disqualified. If he could have seen the ball well enough to identify it—even with the aid of binoculars, which I've used several times to identify balls in less-than-ideal locations—Faldo could have taken an unplayable-lie drop. But since he didn't identify the ball, the ball was technically lost, and he took an improper drop that resulted in disqualification.

In recent years some players have taken advantage of their gallery in helping identify their balls. In the 1998 PGA Championship at Sahalee Country Club in Washington, Olin Browne's tee shot on the eighth hole struck a Douglas fir and never came out. Like Faldo, Browne could see a ball, but he couldn't identify it, and there didn't seem to be any way to climb the tree to make a positive ID. No one in the gallery had a pair of binoculars, which Browne could have borrowed and used under the rules, but there were a couple of hardy young men who volunteered to help.

Browne declared the ball unplayable. Then Ken Betzler, a thirty-one-year-old from Seattle, stood on the shoulders of another fan, John Marnin of Portland, and climbed the tree far enough to dislodge Browne's ball. Once the ball was on the ground Browne positively identified it and played on. It didn't help much though. Browne made double bogey on the hole, and never factored in the tournament.

Olin Browne had a little help retrieving his ball from a tree at the 1997 PGA Championship at Sahalee, but Browne failed to capitalize on the assist. He missed the cut. ASSOCIATED PRESS/AP

The only spots on the course where identifying your ball isn't a requirement are the hazards. If you're playing a ball from a hazard—a sand trap, a water hazard, or a ditch or other area deemed by the Committee to be a hazard—you don't have to identify it.

I can't tell you the number of times I've hit balls into the lips of bunkers and the soft sand has completely covered my ball. If I hadn't had a gallery or a marshal nearby I would have certainly lost the ball, but with the aid of others pointing to the spot where the ball entered, I knew I could at least remove enough sand to see a portion of the ball. **Rule 12-1** states in part:

> **In a hazard, if a ball is believed to be covered by loose impediments or sand, the player may remove by probing, raking or other means as much thereof as will enable him to see a part of a ball. If an excess is removed, no penalty is incurred and the ball shall be re-covered so that only a part of the ball is visible. If the ball is moved in such removal, no penalty is incurred; the ball shall be replaced and, if necessary, re-covered.**

Even though you can't ground your club in a hazard, probing the sand with the head of a wedge is perfectly acceptable in this circumstance, but I always use my finger or a rake, lightly removing just enough of the sand to see a portion of the ball. Since I don't have to identify it, I then play the shot. On a few occasions, I've hit the wrong ball (obviously I wasn't the only one who found that particular soft spot in the bunker), but since there is no penalty for playing a wrong ball from a hazard, I continued to probe until my ball was found.

To ensure that you don't have any problems identifying your ball, you should always mark it with a pen in such a way that you can positively identify it as yours. It seems like a silly ritual (and at times players take it to extremes, painting smiley faces or writing verses of Scripture on the their balls) but identifying your ball as yours is critical.

I see it all the time in pro-ams, or playing with my friends at Bay Hill and Latrobe. A guy hits a Callaway 3 into the bushes, marches over to the spot where his ball should be, and finds two Callaway 3s. He didn't mark his ball, so he can't tell which is his. Usually he comes out smiling, saying, "Hey, I found another ball, but it's just like mine. What should I do, Arnie?"

The smile fades when I impart the bad news. If he can't positively identify one of the balls as his, he has to take a lost ball penalty, even though he more than likely found his ball and one other. It seems harsh, but identifying your ball is a fundamental rule of golf. Get in the habit of doing it, and you shouldn't have a problem.

Ball Played as It Lies

Perhaps the oldest axiom in golf, and the one that gets repeated most often, is "You play the ball as it lies." If you hit it in a bad spot, you are responsible for going into the bad spot and hitting it back out without rolling, nudging, kicking, or in any way improving the lie of the ball or the lay of the land. It was one of golf's first rules, and, unfortunately, it's one of the game's most broken rules as well.

You can't go to a club in America, regardless of location or time of year, where you won't find someone playing so-called winter rules. Sometimes it's referred to as "playing the ball up," or "rolling it." On the tour we sometimes play "lift, clean, and place" rules, or "lift, clean, and cheat," as many of the older pros refer to it. This is an exception to the rules that allow a ball in its own fairway to be lifted, cleaned, and replaced as near as possible to its original spot on the ground without penalty. In professional events lift, clean, and cheat (I mean, "place") rules are reserved for wet-weather conditions when mud and debris are likely to be on balls hit in the fairway. In my opinion they are applied too often to compensate for anything less than pristine, perfect playing conditions. The fairways are a little thin? Just invoke the lift, clean, and place rule. A few too many sand-filled divots out there? Pick it up and place it. We've opened Pandora's box by allowing players to put their hands on the ball too often. I just hope it is a trend we can reverse.

Sergio Garcia ran afoul of Rule 13 in the 2001 International when he reached down, spotted, and picked up his ball in the eighth fairway on Saturday. The previous two days, the tournament at Castle Pines had been played under lift, clean, and place rules, but, according to officials, the course had dried out enough by Saturday to play the ball according to the rules. Sergio forgot, and picked up his ball, costing him a penalty shot and bogey on the par-five.

"As soon as I touched it I knew I made a mistake," Sergio said afterward.

Later that same day Andrew Magee was penalized on the 17th fairway for doing the same thing. It seems that habits like handling the ball in the fairways are hard to break.

Other aspects of Rule 13 aren't as straightforward as the general statement of "play the ball as it lies." There are plenty of subtleties to the rule, and, as countless pros have found over the years, plenty of room for error.

The officials who wrote the rule did their best to spell everything out. Rule 13-2 reads like the rules of conduct for a Catholic school cafeteria. Still, people screw it up. The rule reads as follows:

One too many lift-clean-and-places and a subsequent penalty stroke left Sergio Garcia feeling a little out of sorts at the International. ASSOCIATED PRESS/AP

Except as provided in the Rules, a player shall not improve or allow to be improved:

- the position or lie of his ball,
- the area of his intended stance or swing,
- his line of play or a reasonable extension of that line beyond the hole, or
- the area in which he is to drop or place a ball

by any of the following actions:
- moving, bending or breaking anything growing or fixed (including immovable obstructions and objects defining out of bounds),
- creating or eliminating irregularities of surface,
- removing or pressing down sand, loose soil, replaced divots or other cut turf placed in position, or
- removing dew, frost or water

except as follows:
- as may occur in fairly taking his stance,
- in making a stroke or the backward movement of his club for a stroke,
- on the teeing ground in creating or eliminating irregularities of surface, or

- **on the putting green in removing sand and loose soil as provided in Rule 16-1a or in repairing damage as provided in Rule 16-1c.**

The club may be grounded only lightly and shall not be pressed on the ground.

The nuances of this rule almost cost South African Darren Fichardt the most important victory of his career. Leading the 2001 South African Tour Championship by four shots through five holes in the final round, Fichardt barely missed the sixth green, leaving himself a putt over a small strip of fringe. The problem came when Fichardt repaired a pitch mark in the fringe between his ball and the hole—a perfectly legal procedure on the putting surface, but a no-no when your ball and the mark you're repairing are not on the green.

The two-shot penalty was assessed on the seventh tee, and Fichardt went on to make three consecutive bogeys right after receiving the bad news. "A two-shot penalty always knocks you, and I had to dig deep after that," Fichardt said. "But the spectators and my family were all cheering me on and I thought, 'Don't give up now. Hang on, you're still in the tournament.'"

Fichardt did hang on to shoot a closing 68 and reclaim his four-shot lead by the time the final putt fell. Afterward he was happy about the win, but he knew what he needed to do to improve his game.

"I've got to learn the rules a little better," he said with a smile.

Darren Fichardt won't soon forget when and where he can repair pitch mark. His mistake regarding that rule almost cost him the South African Tour Championship. ASSOCIATED PRESS/AP

Another prominent incident involving Rule 13 occurred at 7:00 A.M. on the Friday morning of the 2001 U.S. Open at Southern Hills in Tulsa, Oklahoma. There had been a rain delay on Thursday, which meant that a fair number of players had to come back on Friday to finish their first rounds. In situations like that, where darkness or bad weather force a suspension of play, players mark their balls, then replace them in the same spot the next morning. It happens all the time.

Which is what made this Friday's situation so unusual. When two-time U.S. Open winner Lee Janzen returned to the ninth fairway to resume his first round, he noticed that the maintenance crew had swept the dew off every spot in the fairway except for one three-foot square where his ball marker was sitting. Janzen assumed that the crew hadn't wanted to disturb his mark, so he thought nothing of taking out his towel and sopping the excess dew from the area before replacing his ball. The rest of the fairway had been swept. What would it hurt to clean the spot around his ball?

"Everything else was clean," Janzen said. "All I did was try to get the same lie. I just wiped it away."

Janzen played the remaining 27½ holes, completing his first and second round on Friday, and entering the weekend at five-over-par, one better than the cut-line.

Throughout the day James Halliday, chairman of the Royal Canadian Golf Association, and Janzen's official for the day, never uttered a word. But, according to USGA officials, Halliday awoke in the middle of the night on Friday night thinking he might have witnessed a violation. He put his concerns in writing and presented them to Tom Meeks, the director of competitions for the USGA, on Saturday morning.

"We read it and had a decision right there on it," Meeks said. "Then I started trying to find Lee."

Janzen had removed dew, a clear violation of Rule 13-2. He had, through his actions, improved the position or lie of the ball as well as the area of his intended swing. The fact that he was simply swatting away a little dew to make his lie the same as everyone else's on the hole was irrelevant. Janzen had broken Rule 13-2.

The rub came from the actions of the official. According to Ernie Els, who played with Janzen on Friday, "The way I see it, if the rules officials see a guy break a rule, tell him on the spot. Come over, show him the rule book, and tell him what the penalty is. Then the guy knows where he stands and what he has to do. We're all professionals. That's the way it should happen."

But that's not the way it happened in this case. After meeting to discuss Halliday's observations and written statement, the USGA initially put out a release stating that Janzen had been disqualified for signing an incorrect scorecard. Minutes later, that was revised. Reed Mackenzie, the USGA vice president and chairman of the Rules of Golf Committee, said, "Ordinarily, when a player fails to incur a penalty and signs for a score lower than should have been recorded, the result is disqualification. But since the committeeman observed the violation and failed to notify the player of the penalty, the penalty of disqualification is waived. However, the penalty strokes must still be added to the score."

Janzen was reached at 9:45 A.M. on Saturday and told that two strokes had been added to his score. Instead of starting the weekend at five-over-par, Janzen was seven-over-par. He had missed the cut. It wasn't a technical disqualification, but the result was the same. Janzen went home on Saturday.

Janzen accepted his fate like the classy man that he is, but he was still a little miffed at not knowing about his infraction a little sooner. Every group in a U.S. Open has a rules official, and Halliday had watched Janzen's every move on Thursday and Friday without uttering a peep. That, Janzen thought, made the penalty a little tougher to swallow.

"PGA Tour officials do this sort of thing every week, and things happen on tour all the time. They're just on top of things. The USGA has a large base of guys out here walking around, but I don't know how many tournaments they cover a year. I guess it would be like trying to play in one or two tournaments a year. You get rusty and you miss things."

But Mackenzie was unapologetic. "If the official makes an error, that's a committee error," he said. "We can't take back the actions and the penalty is applied. In a perfect world, it would have been applied on the spot. But we don't have a separate set of rules for two-time U.S. Open winners. I don't feel at all guilty. It was unfortunate that I didn't catch it earlier, but Mr. Janzen breached the rules."

Janzen didn't argue the point, but he did say that he might have played the last 27 holes a little differently had he known the situation. "I would have been two strokes higher, and who knows what would have happened," he said. "But at least I would have had the opportunity to rectify my position.

"What was funny is that the second time we came down nine fairway, [MacKenzie] was carrying a briefcase. I said, 'What do you have in there, the decisions book?' He said, 'Yeah, I carry it everywhere. The Rules and the Decisions.'"

Too bad Mackenzie didn't catch up on his reading while Janzen still had a chance.

Lee Janzen wasn't too pleased by the late ruling he got in the 2001 U.S. Open Championship. Janzen was penalized a day after the fact for mopping dew off the ground. The penalty forced him to miss the cut in the championship. ASSOCIATED PRESS/AP

Another of golf's most famous rulings involved the next section of Rule 13—**Rule 13-3**, which reads:

A player is entitled to place his feet firmly in taking his stance, but he shall not build a stance.

At the 1987 Andy Williams San Diego Open, Craig Stadler got an education on exactly what "building a stance" entails under the rules. During Saturday's third round, Stadler pushed his tee shot on the 14th hole, and the ball came to rest under a pine tree. The ground was muddy from some earlier rain, but mud was the least of Stadler's worries. The only shot he had was to kneel and try to swing under the branches of the tree. Because of the mud, and the fact that Stadler was wearing light-colored pants, he placed a towel on the ground to protect the knees of his trousers, then knelt down and punched the ball back to the fairway.

The following day Stadler finished the tournament with a 270 total and walked to the scorer's tent assuming he had finished second. Instead he was told he had been disqualified. Stadler's towel had violated Rule 13-3. He had built a stance. The penalty for the infraction should have been two shots, but Stadler didn't add the two shots to his Saturday score, and thus signed an incorrect scorecard.

The ruling was correct, but Stadler got a raw deal. He got the only revenge he was looking for in 1995 when the pine tree on the 14th hole contracted a fungus. At the club's invitation Stadler traveled to San Diego and sawed the tree down. He never felt better.

Paul Azinger also ran afoul of Rule 13 and received golf's ultimate penalty. This one occurred in the first round of the 1991 Doral-Ryder Open in Miami, when Azinger attempted to play a shot out of the edge of the lake that borders the 18th hole. The ball was slightly submerged, so Azinger carefully took his stance and prepared to blast it back to the fairway. In the process, he pawed the ground with his left foot, dislodging a small rock.

Rule 13-4 reads in part:

> **Except as provided in the Rules, before making a stroke at a ball which is in a hazard (whether a bunker or a water hazard) or which, having been lifted from a hazard, may be dropped or placed in the hazard, the player shall not:**
>
> **a. Test the condition of the hazard or any similar hazard,**
> **b. Touch the ground in the hazard or water in the water hazard with a club or otherwise, or**
> **c. Touch or move a loose impediment lying in or touching the hazard.**

Azinger had removed a loose impediment by pawing at it with his foot. But he didn't know it at the time, and neither did any of the rules officials on the scene. It wasn't until Friday afternoon when a television viewer called that anyone at the tournament

Building a stance cost Azinger a chance at a win in Miami. ASSOCIATED PRESS/AP

knew there had been a violation. By then, Azinger had shot a second round 65 to pull within a shot of the lead.

Rather than having tour officials shuffle Azinger to the media tent to answer questions after his round, Mike Shea, one of the tour's senior rules officials, escorted him to a CBS television truck where they all watched a tape of Thursday's incident. Azinger admitted he had removed the impediment, and took his punishment. He had signed an incorrect scorecard on Thursday because he hadn't added the two shots for the penalty at 18. Rather than entering the weekend one shot off the lead, Azinger drove home to Orlando, having been disqualified.

Isao Aoki was also disqualified because of his ignorance of Rule 13-4. While leading the 1994 Doug Sanders Celebrity Classic, Aoki hit a ball under the lip of a fairway bunker, and the ball could not be easily found. Both Aoki and his caddie walked through the bunker looking for the ball, and, when they finally found it, Aoki declared it unplayable. Under the rules, you can take relief from an unplayable lie in the bunker, but you must drop in the bunker.

Aoki stayed put, but he and his caddie raked the footprints they had made in the search. That, it turned out, is a violation of Rule 13-4. Aoki had improved his lie in the hazard. Unaware of the infraction and the two-stroke penalty he should have taken, Aoki signed for a 68, and was disqualified for signing an incorrect card.

Isao Aoki's bunker mistake cost him a penalty in 1994. ASSOCIATED PRESS/AP

I feel somewhat responsible for some of the wording of Rule 13-4. As is often the case, rules incidents that arise in major championships spark debate among golf's ruling bodies, and a change is written into the rules. That's exactly what happened after I grounded my club in a hazard in Augusta in 1968.

I was on the par-five second hole, and had just hit my second shot into the greenside bunker. It was a long trap shot and I didn't have a very good lie. I took as full a swing as I could, but failed to get the ball out of the sand. In frustration, I did what I do a lot after a poor shot: I took a practice swing. Only this time my practice swing was in the sand trap, and I hit the sand with my club even though I still had a shot to play from the bunker.

I've had plenty of questionable rulings regarding when and how to drop in and play from a bunker throughout my career. ASSOCIATED PRESS/AP

At the time, Jack Tuthill, the rules officials on the scene, told me I had, in fact, grounded my club in a hazard, and he gave me a two-shot penalty. But my good friend Doc Giffin, who was in the gallery at the time, knew that the exact same thing had happened to Kel Nagle in the Houston Open, and tour officials had ruled that there was no penalty. Doc wanted to make sure that Jack's ruling was correct, so he approached Frank Hannigan, one of the senior rules officials and future executive director of the USGA. Hannigan and Jack caucused on the fourth hole and determined that my actions, as the rules were written, did not constitute grounding the club in a hazard and my two-stroke penalty was rescinded. Since I had already hit the sand once in taking my shot, they ruled that taking another swing didn't constitute grounding my club in a hazard.

Shortly after that incident, the USGA modified Rule 13-4, and such an action became a violation.

Karrie Webb found that out the hard way at the 2000 Firstar LPGA Classic. Leading by a shot in the final round, Webb hit her second shot at the par-five eighth hole in the greenside bunker, just as I had done at number two at Augusta almost four decades before. And just as I had done, Webb left her third shot in the sand. Staying true to the Palmer form, Webb then took a practice whack at the sand. Only this time, it was a two-shot penalty.

"I forgot the ball was still in the bunker and I was just practicing," Webb said. "I knew immediately it was a penalty. I told my caddie, 'If I'd thought about getting a two-shot penalty, I would have taken a bigger cut at it.'"

Karrie Webb's practice stroke at the Firstar LPGA Classic cost her a chance at the title. MICHAEL C. COHEN

Webb took a triple-bogey eight on the hole, and lost the tournament by one shot to Annika Sorenstam. If Karrie had been playing back in the 1960s, she would have been fine, but in the new millennium her actions cost her a tournament win. What a difference forty years makes.

Larry Nelson knew he could hit his ball off the bridge at the Tradition, but he had to ask for a few clarifications on grounding his club. ASSOCIATED PRESS/AP

Larry Nelson has been around long enough to know the rules, so it surprised many spectators at the final round of the Tradition, one of the senior tour's major championships, when Nelson grounded his club on the wooden bridge that crosses the water hazard at the par-five 15th hole. Rules aficionados know that the boundaries of a hazard extended upward and down-ward, and there was no question that Nelson was in the hazard. Wasn't that a violation of Rule 13-4?

Not at all. Nelson knew enough to ask an official, who informed him that a bridge crossing a hazard was classified as an "obstruc-tion" inside the hazard, and the rules allowed Nelson to ground his club on an obstruction. He had to be careful not to remove any loose impediments from the bridge—like rocks or leaves—since that would have been a violation, but he was able to take a couple of practice swings, and ground his club at address. Nelson proceeded to make par on the fifth, and, in the process, teach everyone in his gallery a valuable lesson about the nuances of Rule 13.

Striking the Ball

In the 500-year history of golf, the rules have gone through many evolutionary changes. Even in the course of my fifty-year career the game has changed, and the rules have been transformed. Rule 14 is a perfect example of how things have evolved in golf over the years.

It should be simple enough. The first part of the rule—**Rule 14-1**—reads:

> **The ball shall be fairly struck at with the head of the club and must not be pushed, scraped or spooned.**

For those of you out there who are movie buffs, all those silly gyrations Kevin Costner went through in *Tin Cup*—hitting the ball with a spade, lying on his belly on the green and using the putter

An entertaining movie starring a nice guy, Kevin Costner's *Tin Cup* had little basis in golf's realities. ASSOCIATED PRESS/AP

grip as a pool cue—are illegal under this rule. In order to make a stroke at the ball you have to strike at the ball with the head of the club without pushing or scaping the ball into the hole. Costner's movie was cute, but a fair bit of it had nothing to do with the game of golf.

While Rule 14-1 has remained reasonably intact over the years, **Rule 14-2** is relatively new. It reads:

In making a stroke, a player shall not:

a. accept physical assistance or protection from the elements, or

b. allow his caddie, his partner, or his partner's caddie to position himself on or close to an extension of the line of play or the line of putt behind the ball.

I have pictures of myself playing in numerous tournaments where my caddie was holding an umbrella over my head as I putted. That was common up through the 1970s, as was having your caddie stand behind the line of your putt. It wasn't until recently that those rules were changed, and rightfully so. A golfer should brave the elements while playing his shots. I took advantage of the old rule when it was in effect, but I have no problem playing by the new one.

Perhaps the most significant and sweeping changes in the rules relate to Rule 14-3. In fact, the underpinnings of this rule are still changing, with new regulations coming out every year or so. The wording of the rule is pretty simple. It reads in part:

**Except as provided in the Rules, during a stipu-
lated round the player shall not use any artificial
device or unusual equipment...**

Seems simple enough until you ask the natural follow-up question: What is "unusual equipment?" That's when things get a little sticky. According to the wording of the rule, unusual equipment
is anything

a. Which might assist him in making a stroke or in his
   play; or

b. For the purpose of gauging or measuring distance or
   conditions which might affect his play; or

c. Which might assist him in gripping the club, except that:

   (i) plain gloves may be worn;

   (ii) resin, powder and drying or moisturizing agents
         may be used; and

   (iii) a towel or handkerchief may be wrapped around
          the grip.

Later, in an Appendix, the rule book attempts to define what is
and what is not considered "conforming" equipment, that is,
equipment that isn't "unusual." But the Appendix is mind-
numbingly technical and constantly changing. Unless you know
what "coefficient of restitution" means or what the "axis of
symmetry" is on the grooves of your clubs, you're probably not
going to be able to follow many of the regulations outlined for
equipment.

I go into many of the equipment issues in the Afterword to this book, but suffice it to say that you aren't alone in your confusion over what is and what is not legal and conforming.

One of the saddest incidents relating to equipment occurred in Orlando at the 1996 Walt Disney World Invitational. On Sunday afternoon, Taylor Smith tapped in a putt to shoot 21-under-par for the week, and, he thought, earn a playoff spot with Tiger Woods, who had also played brilliantly. There was only one problem. Smith had played using a nonconforming putter.

Long putters—the kind that players either stick in their chests or harness under their chins—are about as odd as anything the rules of golf allow, but they aren't technically considered "unusual." You can putt with a broom handle putter if you want. But if you have two grips on that putter, as Smith did, they both must be circular in cross-section. That's different from the rule for standard putters with only one grip, so it's easy to see how Smith or anyone else could become confused.

Smith had re-gripped his long putter, adding two paddle grips (those with one flat side) to the shaft. During Sunday's final round, Smith's playing companion, Lennie Clements, informed PGA Tour official Arvin Ginn of a possible infraction. Clements knew the rule, and he knew that Smith's putter didn't conform.

Tour officials agreed. On the ninth hole, Smith was informed that he had possibly violated a rule. Officials wanted to be sure before making it official, but there was a good chance that Smith would be disqualified. He pressed on, and finished the tournament with the lowest aggregate score in the field. But rather than head back out for a playoff, Smith was given the bad news by Ginn and Mark Russell.

"It wasn't just bad," Russell said. "It was awful. He'd made a mistake by putting non-conforming grips on his putter, and we had no choice but to disqualify him. It was tough, and it was sad."

Even Tiger, who benefited from the ruling by being declared the outright winner, felt sorry for Smith. But the rules were clear. Smith's grips were considered "illegal," and the penalty for using them was disqualification.

Assuming you are striking the ball with the head of the club and doing so with something other than "unusual" equipment, there are a few other pitfalls you need to avoid to remain in compliance with Rule 14. The first—**Rule 14-4**—says you can't hit the ball more than once with a single stroke. The exact wording is:

> **If a player's club strikes the ball more than once in the course of a stroke, the player shall count the stroke and add a penalty stroke, making two strokes in all.**

The most famous application of this rule came in the 1985 U.S. Open. That year, Taiwan's T. C. Chen, a former sailor in the Chinese navy, held a two shot lead over Andy North going into the final round. Chen had already made history in the second round by recording the only double-eagle ever recorded in a U.S. Open on the 527-yard par-five second hole at Oakland Hills Country Club in Michigan. Two days later, he would make history again.

T. C. Chen's double chip at the 1985 U.S. Open forever gave him the nickname "Two-Chip Chen." BRIAN MORGAN

Through four holes on Sunday, Chen had extended his lead to four shots over North, and looked to be in complete control of the championship. Then, at the par-four fifth, he pushed his approach shot into the deep rough thirty yards right of the green. Chen left his pitch shot short, still in the deep stuff. He left himself a delicate pitch from three-inch rough to a closely cut pin. It was a shot in which anything could happen.

Chen's long, fluid stroke wasn't suited for U.S. Open rough, where hacking the ball out is the order of the day. For his fourth shot at the fifth, he took a long stroke, and, as is often the case in long grass, the rough grabbed the club. The ball didn't jump out the way Chen had expected, and suddenly, in the blink of an eye, the club head of his wedge hit the ball in midair, flipping it onto the collar of the green. In accordance with Rule 14-4, Chen received a one shot penalty for hitting the ball twice, and he took a quadruple bogey eight on the hole.

He never recovered and Andy North won the 1985 U.S. Open. Since that day, T. C. Chen has been known as Two-Chip Chen, a cruel moniker because of one of the most infamous shots in U.S. Open history.

Wrong Ball

Rule 15 defines and sets penalties for playing a wrong ball. In essence a wrong ball is any ball you hit that isn't the ball you teed off with, unless you have replaced your original ball in accordance with the rules, or hit a provisional or "second" ball.

If you hit the wrong ball, you're penalized. In stroke play the penalty is two shots, and in match play it's loss of hole. The only exception to that is when you hit the wrong ball from a hazard. Since you aren't required to identify your ball in a hazard, if you take a swing at a ball you believe to be yours and discover later that you've hit the wrong ball, there is no penalty, but you have to return to the hazard and either play the correct ball or take the appropriate drop.

You seldom see professionals play wrong balls. Not that we are any smarter than average golfers; we simply have spotters, marshals, forecaddies, gallery members, and caddies to point us in the right direction. But even all those safeguards don't prevent all problems. In the 1998 Cisco World Match Play Championships,

Colin Montgomerie and Thomas Bjorn drove the ball side by side in the rough on the par-four seventh. Because the tee shot is blind, spotters were in the fairway to mark the balls, but when the players arrived, the spotters had gotten it backward. The spotter with the big red "M" for Montgomerie was standing beside Bjorn's ball, and vice versa. Montgomerie hit the wrong ball and lost the hole. Fortunately the incident didn't affect the outcome of the match. Montgomerie defeated Bjorn 4 and 3 and advanced to the quarterfinals.

Tony Jacklin also played a wrong ball in the 2001 Senior British Open at Royal County Down. On the second hole of the opening round, Jacklin hooked his drive into a stand of thick Irish rough. Jacklin found a ball and played it without identifying it. When he got to it he realized he had hit the wrong ball. The two-stroke penalty led to a disastrous 76 and, ultimately, a missed cut for Jacklin.

"It was not the nicest thing to happen in my first competitive round at County Down," Jacklin said afterward.

One of my favorite "wrong ball" stories never really happened except in literature and on film. It comes from the Ian Fleming book *Goldfinger*, which was later made into a movie starring Sean Connery as James Bond. Both the book and the movie depict a golf match between Bond and his evil nemesis, Auric Goldfinger, at the Stoke Poges Club north of London. The wager is a solid gold bar.

Through 16 holes the match is even, but on 17 Bond hits a great drive while Goldfinger pulls his ball into the rough. After a frantic

Sir Sean Connery, an avid golfer, had one of Hollywood's best golf scenes in the film *Goldfinger*. ASSOCIATED PRESS/HO

search for the ball by Goldfinger and his caddie and manservant, Oddjob, it appears as though Goldfinger will have to take a lost ball. But Oddjob cheats, dropping a ball down his trousers through a hole in his pocket, then claiming it belongs to Goldfinger.

Bond knows it's a different ball, because he is standing on the original ball a few yards away. But the savvy agent says nothing, and the two men halve 17. Bond then plays a trick on Goldfinger. When 007 reaches into the cup to retrieve Goldfinger's ball after the putt to halve falls in at 17, the agent changes balls, replacing the Slazinger #1 with a Slazinger #7.

After Goldfinger tees off on 18 with the new ball (the "wrong" ball), Bond has him. At the end of the 18th hole, Bond calls Goldfinger for playing the wrong ball. The penalty is a loss of the 18th hole, and the gold bar, worth about $12,000 in the early 1960s when the book and movie came out. Of course, had Goldfinger declared that he was changing balls at the end of the 17th, no penalty would have occurred, but because he continued play with the same ball (the wrong ball), the disastrous penalty was effected and the plot of the movie thickened.

Both men actually cheated—Goldfinger for dropping a ball and claiming it to be his original, and Bond for switching balls on his opponent—but it's still a nifty story. It's also one of the few times Hollywood got a golf story right by citing Rule 15 and its appropriate penalty.

There are a few times when the wrong ball rule applies to situations in which a player would love to play his original ball, but can't. Such was the case for Scotland's Raymond Russell, who was looking to finish in the top ten of the 2001 Compass English Open when he was forced to play a "wrong ball."

It happened on the 17th green at the Marriott Forest of Arden course when Russell marked his ball and tossed it to his caddie, Clark Ingram. But Ingram couldn't handle the toss, and the ball tumbled off the front of the green and into a water hazard. The two men searched feverishly in the water for the original ball, but couldn't find it. Ingram even took off his shoes and waded into the pond in the hopes of stepping on the ball or otherwise stumbling across it. But it was futile. The original ball was gone.

Russell would have to replace the ball, which violated **Rule 15-1**, which reads:

> **A player must hole out with the ball played from the teeing ground unless a Rule permits him to substitute another ball. If a player substitutes another ball when not so permitted, that ball is not a wrong ball; it becomes the ball in play and, if the error is not corrected as provided in Rule 20-6, the player shall incur a penalty of loss of hole in match play or two strokes in stroke play.**

Russell and Ingram would have loved to correct the error, but they couldn't. Russell had to replace the ball he couldn't find, thus incurring a two-stroke penalty under Rule 15-1.

The Putting Green

Things are a little different once your ball is on the green. For one thing, you can mark it, pick it up, and clean it, a rule that went into effect in the 1950s with the advent of irrigation. Once you could water a golf course, balls picked up mud a lot easier, which led to players being able to mark and clean their balls on the green.

It also led to some questionable rules issues. Dave Hill, an opinionated tour player who had some success in the late 1960s and 1970s, was the first pro to publicly accuse his fellow professionals of cheating on the greens by fudging their marks. Hill didn't name names, saying, "They know who they are." I've always thought it was an outrageous accusation. I don't know of a single professional who cheats, whether it's kicking a ball in the rough, or nudging a spot forward on the green. It was unprofessional of Dave Hill to say such things twenty-five years ago, and it's uncommon for pros to make similar accusations today.

There are only a couple of incidents where marking a golf ball has been called into question. The most memorable one in my book was the accusation made by Sweden's Jarmo Sandelin at the 1998 Trophee Lancome in Paris. Sandelin can be politely called "eccentric," although he's been called much worse by his fellow European Tour players. He's the only player in European Tour history to be cited for a dress code violation for wearing a see-through, fishnet shirt in an event, and he's one of the few players ever threatened by Phil Mickelson. Mickelson was playing with Sandelin in the 1996 Alfred Dunhill Cup when Sandelin put his putter to his shoulder like a machine gun and rattled off some mock shots in Mickelson's direction. The American was having none of it. Mickelson put his nose a millimeter away from Sandelin's forehead and explained in unambiguous terms that such actions were unacceptable. So it came as no surprise to many of Sandelin's peers when the Swede accused Mark O'Meara of cheating by improperly marking his ball in the Trophee Lancome.

O'Meara is one of the most honest, hardworking men in golf and his integrity is beyond reproach, but that didn't stop Sandelin from saying O'Meara violated the rules. The specific rule in question was **Rule 16-1b**, which states:

> **A ball on the putting green may be lifted and, if desired, cleaned. A ball so lifted shall be replaced on the spot from which it was lifted.**

Mark O'Meara's mark at the Trophee Lancome stirred some controversy, but resulted in a proper ruling. MICHAEL C. COHEN

Sandelin said O'Meara marked his ball, but replaced it in a spot a fraction of an inch forward from its original position. He even produced videotape of the incident, claiming the tape clearly showed O'Meara spotting a ball in one spot and replacing it in another spot, infinitesimally closer to the hole. O'Meara had made the three-footer in question, and gone on to win the golf tournament with Sandelin finishing second. But Sandelin challenged O'Meara to return the trophy and the winner's check, saying it had been "fraudulently obtained."

A committee of European Tour executives met, examined the tapes, and discussed the issue. They determined that O'Meara had won fair and square, and no further action would be taken. But Sandelin wouldn't let it die, which angered his fellow professionals on both sides of the pond. O'Meara even appeared on the Golf Channel to defend himself, examining the tape with Peter Kessler and saying that if, indeed, he had spotted the ball ahead of its original position (as the tape seemed to indicate) it was by no more than a millimeter, and was certainly unintentional. The incident was soon dropped.

The only other miss-marked violation worth mentioning occurred in 1972 when Jane Blalock was accused of cheating in the second round of the Women's Bluegrass Invitational in Louisville, Kentucky. According to accounts at the time, Blalock was said to have "inchwormed" her ball out of a footprint by marking it in one spot, and replacing it in another. The five-woman LPGA executive committee disqualified her that evening.

Jane Blalock was accused of "inchworming" her ball forward on the greens. The charges were never proved, and Blalock won a lawsuit against the LPGA.
MICHAEL C. COHEN

Later, twenty-nine players signed a petition calling for Blalock to be suspended from the LPGA for the remainder of the season. She just so happened to be the leading money winner at the time with two victories in the early months of the season.

While the charges were never substantiated, Blalock sued the LPGA on antitrust grounds, and won a $13,500 judgment and $90,000 in legal fees. As a result of that case, the LPGA created the position of tour commissioner to moderate and oversee disputes between players. Blalock remains adamant in her denials concerning the cheating allegations, but, as she wrote in her 1977 autobiography, *The Guts to Win*, "people will always have their doubts."

Of course, other parts of Rule 16 are broken quite regularly. I broke one in the 1999 U.S. Senior Open when, in disgust at my abysmal play, I hurriedly tapped in a putt by straddling the line. That was a violation of **Rule 16-1e**, which reads:

> **The player shall not make a stroke on the putting green from a stance astride, or with either foot touching, the line of the putt or an extension of that line behind the ball.**

For a number of years we referred to Rule 16-1e as the "Sam Snead Rule." When Sam's putting got so bad he couldn't draw the putter back, he started facing the hole and putting between his legs like a croquet stroke. That, the USGA decided, gave Sam an unfair advantage over the field, so they wrote and installed Rule 16-1e, even though Sam was one of the only players to putt standing "astride" of the hole.

I did it out of frustration and without thinking. With the two-shot penalty I made a quadruple bogey on the last hole and shot 84, an embarrassing ending to an embarrassing day.

Pitiful play on my part was no excuse for the bone-headed error I made on the 18th green at the 1999 Senior U.S. Open. ASSOCIATED PRESS/AP

Jesper Parnevik also ran afoul of one of the sections of Rule 16, and it took a caddie to call Parnevik on it. It happened on Hilton Head at one of my favorite tournaments, The Heritage Classic. The Bermuda greens at Harbour Town are small, and the course puts a premium on precision iron play, so it stood to reason that Parnevik, a great iron player, should do quite well. But on the par-three 17th during the second round, the Swede made an unfortunate error.

After hitting the testy green, Parnevik noticed seedpods scattered along the line of his putt. Seedpods are natural objects and are considered loose impediments. They can be removed on the putting surface. But **Rule 16-1a** puts limits on exactly how those loose impediments may be removed. The rule reads in part:

16-1 General
a. Touching Line of Putt
The line of putt must not be touched except:
(i) the player may move sand and loose soil on the putting green and other loose impediments by picking them up or by brushing them aside with his hand or a club without pressing anything down.

Parnevik had taken off his glove after hitting the green, and he used it to brush away the seedpods. The glove, if it's not on your hand, cannot be used as a broom. Parnevik was in violation of Rule 16-1a.

Jesper Parnevik has always been known for his clothing, but using his golf glove as a broom cost him at the MCI Heritage Classic. ASSOCIATED PRESS/CP

A television viewer didn't spot the incident, but a member of the gallery did report it to officials after the round. By then it was too late. Parnevik had already signed his card. Plus, he couldn't remember how he had brushed the seedpods away. He was thinking about his putt, not the housekeeping duties he had performed ahead of time. Parnevik's caddie remembered the incident and, when questioned, reported that Parnevik had, indeed, brushed the loose impediments aside with his glove. Because he had already signed a scorecard that didn't include the required two-shot penalty, Parnevik was disqualified.

If Rule 16-1e is the "Sam Snead Rule" then you would have to call **Rule 16-2** the "Don January Rule." It reads:

> **When any part of the ball overhangs the lip of the hole, the player is allowed enough time to reach the hole without unreasonable delay and an additional ten seconds to determine whether the ball is at rest. If by then the ball has not fallen into the hole, it is deemed to be at rest. If the ball subsequently falls into the hole, the player is deemed to have holed out with his last stroke, and he shall add a penalty stroke to his score for the hole; otherwise there is no penalty under this Rule.**

Don January stood around for eight minutes while his ball overhung the cup in 1963. The rule book was changed shortly afterward. ASSOCIATED PRESS/AP

In the 1963 Phoenix Open, Don January had a putt roll up to the lip of the hole and stop, seemingly defying gravity. January walked up and examined the ball, then informed his fellow competitors that he could not tap in because the ball was still moving. He was certain it was moving, ever so slightly. Hitting a moving ball is against the rules, so January couldn't tap in.

He waited, and waited, and waited for seven agonizing minutes with the gallery groaning and the players behind him yelling for him to get out of the way. Finally, the ball fell into the cup, and January said, "Told you it was moving."

That incident prompted the USGA and R&A to write Rule 16-2 in 1964 limiting the amount of time a player can wait for a ball overhanging the hole to fall in.

The first penalty ever assessed under the new rule came in 1965, a year after it was written. During the second round of the Colonial National Invitational in Fort Worth, Texas, Tommy Bolt's ball hung on the lip of the 14th hole for two minutes before falling in. Bolt was penalized two shots (the penalty is one shot now) and subsequently informed tour officials what he thought of their new rule.

There have been many instances where Rule 16-2 has been applied, some in the midst of great controversy. In the 1998 NEC World Series of Golf, Lee Janzen hit a ball over the lip of the 17th hole in the first round. Janzen walked up and surveyed the ball, then turned and spoke to his playing partner, Vijay Singh, who also

Tommy Bolt was the first PGA Tour player penalized under the new rule stating that a ball overhanging a hole is deemed to be at rest after ten seconds.
ASSOCIATED PRESS/AP

Meg Mallon let a ball hang over the lip a little too long and the resulting penalty cost her. ASSOCIATED PRESS/AP

walked over and looked at the ball. About twenty seconds passed before Janzen started to tap the ball in, only to have it fall into the hole. After the round Janzen signed for a three on the 17th rather than the four he would have made if he had added the appropriate one-shot penalty.

Viewers who saw the incident on television called tour officials, who reviewed tapes and agreed that Janzen had, indeed, violated Rule 16-2. Because he had already signed his scorecard for a lower score, Janzen was disqualified. The disqualification later proved significant, because it dropped Janzen out of the top ten in President's Cup points for the year. Had Hal Sutton not withdrawn from the President's Cup because of a death in the family, Janzen wouldn't have made the team.

This also rekindled the debate over whether television should be used as a vehicle for enforcing the rules. There are strong opinions on both sides, but I find the trend troubling. Rarely does a week go by when someone doesn't call the tournament office of this or that event swearing that he saw a rules violation. I fear that we've created an interactive environment in which golf fans are no longer content to be spectators. They want to inject themselves into the competition by becoming armchair rules officials. Sure, the rules should be enforced, but I'm uncomfortable with having television audiences as the enforcers.

Meg Mallon was disqualified after the first round of the 1996 Jamie Farr Kroger Classic for waiting 18 or so seconds for a putt to fall in, then signing an incorrect scorecard, having not taken the appropriate penalty. Even though Mallon would have been leading the golf tournament, she never uttered a peep about her disqualification, even though there were no television cameras anywhere around. The rules were enforced because honorable people were honest and forthright in telling officials what had happened. And no cameras or instant replays were required.

Brian Gay got hit with the blunt end of our television ruling mentality in the 2000 Honda Classic in Fort Lauderdale. While putting on the 17th green on Sunday, Gay, who was in second place in the golf tournament, had a putt roll up the lip. He calmly walked up to the ball and waited a short amount of time. The ball fell in, and everyone, including me, thought that Gay had made birdie.

Brian Gay saw the best finish of his career jeopardized when a television viewer put a stopwatch on his ball as it overhung the lip. MICHAEL C. COHEN

But some television viewer called in having claimed he put a stopwatch on it. According to the armchair official, Gay had waited three seconds too long. PGA Tour rules official Slugger White viewed the tapes himself, and agreed. With watch in hand, White concluded that Gay had waited three seconds too long and should add a penalty stroke to his score at 17.

This is where the rule gets a little fuzzy. Brian Gay is not a very emotional player. He goes about his business quickly and professionally. After the putt on 17, he immediately walked up to the hole to examine his ball. Under Rule 16-2, he was allowed a "reasonable amount of time" to reach his ball. If Gay had fallen to his knees and groaned in agony at having so narrowly missed such a critical birdie putt, then, slowly righted himself and waved to the crowd before walking up to the ball, he would have been well within the ten-second time-limit. Being a fast player cost Gay one shot and $88,943 in prize money.

The Flagstick

Another relatively new rule concerns the attendance and removal of the flagstick. There was a time, not too long ago for a guy in his seventies, when if a player was on the green and no one was around to attend the flagstick, the player could play his shot without fear of a penalty. Hitting the flagstick, even on the green, was okay under those circumstances. All that has changed now. **Rule 17-3** reads:

> **The player's ball shall not strike:**
>
> **a. The flagstick when attended, removed or held up by the player, his partner or either of their caddies, or by another person with the player's authority or prior knowledge; or**
>
> **b. The player's caddie, his partner or his partner's caddie when attending the flagstick, or**

another person attending the flagstick with the player's authority or prior knowledge or anything carried by such person; or

c. The flagstick in the hole, unattended, when the ball has been played from the putting green.

Most of that gobbledygook can be summed up pretty easily. You can't hit somebody attending the flag for you, or the flagstick being held up. You don't want players using the flagstick or their caddies as backstops.

Rule 17-3c is where amateurs sometimes get into trouble. You're on the green, your buddies are messing around off to the side, and you have a lengthy putt that you're ready to hit. Even if the flagstick (it's never called a "pin" in the rule book) is in the hole, you're likely going to go ahead and putt to keep things moving along. Under a strict interpretation of Rule 17-3c, however, if your ball hits the flagstick under those conditions, you're penalized two shots.

I liked this one the old way. If no one is around to attend the stick—something that would never happen in a professional tournament, and would rarely happen in competition at the highest amateur levels—then you should be allowed to proceed on the green without fear of a penalty. There's no competitive advantage gained by putting at the flag. If anything, you risk having a putt hit the flagstick and bounce out that might have otherwise gone in the hole.

I've never been penalized for hitting the flagstick while putting, but only because I hit some putts that had no chance of going in. During a Shell Wonderful World of Golf match between Jack Nicklaus and me on the King and the Bear Course at the World Golf Village in St. Augustine, Florida, I came as close as I ever have to incurring a penalty for hitting the pin, and as close as I've come to banning my architectural partner, Ed Seay, from any future duties as a caddie.

Ed was my caddie for the made-for-TV event in March 2001 when, during a critical birdie putt, I had Ed attend the flagstick. But when I struck my putt, Ed couldn't get the flag out of the hole. As the putt rolled closer, Ed began to panic. If the ball hit the flagstick I would be assessed a two-shot penalty. He tried to keep his cool, while pulling and twisting and yanking on the flagstick as hard as he could. Ed's a big man, and he was putting everything he had into the effort.

Then, just as my ball reached the hole, Ed gave the flagstick one more yank, and the entire cup came up out of the ground.

Fortunately, my ball missed the hole. Ed was off the hook as far as penalties were concerned, but he took a mighty hard razzing from the rest of the group for the remainder of the round.

Ball at Rest Moved

This is the rule players have most often broken when you hear or read about them calling penalties on themselves. Under certain conditions, if a ball moves, the player is deemed to have moved it and there's a one-stroke penalty. Most of the time the only person who could possibly see the minute movement of a ball in those circumstances is the player himself. That's why you'll often hear about a player calling a one-shot penalty on himself even though no one witnessed any rules violation.

Of course it's not always the player's fault when a ball moves. In the Buick Challenge, Steve Pate was walking up the 16th fairway when a dog ran out from the woods on the right side of the fairway and snatched his ball. The offending mutt scampered around the edge of the rough for a few seconds before dropping the ball and wagging his tail. In that case, the ball was moved by an "outside agency"—the dog—and according to **Rule 18-1**:

If a ball at rest is moved by an outside agency, the player shall incur no penalty and the ball shall be replaced before the player plays another stroke.

Pate took a drop as near as possible to the ball's original position and played on without penalty.

Steve Pate didn't chase down the dog that nabbed his golf ball, but under the rules he didn't have to. ASSOCIATED PRESS/AP

Where the penalties start accruing is when a ball at rest moves after you have addressed it. Rule 18-2b reads:

If a player's ball in play moves after he has addressed it (other than as a result of a stroke), the player shall be deemed to have moved the ball and shall incur a penalty stroke. The player shall replace the ball unless the movement of the ball occurs after he has begun his swing and he does not discontinue his swing.

We see this a lot on the greens. A player will address his putt, and the ball will move slightly, either falling into a slight depression or wriggling down an incline. As green speeds have increased over the years, the likelihood of the ball moving on the greens has gone up considerably. That's why so many tour players call penalties on themselves for balls moving on the greens.

The rule was an eye-opener for one thirteen-year-old amateur, however. Aree Song Wongluekiet, the golf prodigy from Bradenton, Florida, played her first major championship in April of 2000 when she and her sister, Naree, were given sponsor's exemptions to the Nabisco Championship. Naree missed the cut, but Aree was actually in second place after the opening round. She went on to have a great weekend, shooting 68-75 for a one-over-par (289) total, good enough for a tie for tenth.

Her score would have been two shots better had it not been for a penalty she received at the 14th hole when her ball moved

Aree Wongluekeit was formally introduced to championship golf at the 2000 Nabisco Championship when she incurred a penalty stroke after her ball moved on the green. ASSOCIATED PRESS/AP

and she failed to replace it. According to LPGA rules official Barb Trammell, "We had a call from the ABC television compound when they were on the fifteenth hole. They asked us to look at something that might be a rules violation. We looked at the tape and determined that the ball moved. Aree had addressed it and it moved one-eighth of an inch. Had she replaced the ball, it would have been a one-stroke penalty."

Aree viewed the tape before signing her scorecard and agreed with the LPGA ruling. She had made birdie on the 14th hole, but the two-shot penalty gave her a bogey. "It's the first time something like that has ever happened to me," she said. "I didn't see it move."

It might have been the first time for the thirteen-year-old, but it certainly won't be the last.

I've called more penalties on myself for a ball moving than I can count, but one has bothered me for years now. In 1960, I was leading the Baton Rouge Open by a considerable margin when I addressed a putt on the back nine. Just as I was about to take my stroke, the ball moved, rolling a hundredth of an inch into a small depression. I stepped back and told my fellow competitors that the ball had moved and I needed to add a stroke; then I stepped up and knocked the ball into the hole.

But I forgot to replace it. The putt was no more than three feet in length, and the ball had only moved a fraction of an inch, but according to the rules I should have replaced it. I didn't, and I signed my card and won the golf tournament. By all rights, I guess that incident tainted the victory since, as a practical matter,

I was happy after winning the Baton Rouge Open in 1960, my third victory of the year, as I'm proudly letting everyone know. It wasn't until years later that I remembered a problem I'd had on one of the greens. By then it was too late. The competition was closed. ASSOCIATED PRESS/AP

I signed an incorrect scorecard and should have been disqualified. But I didn't realize what I'd done at the time, and nobody else did either.

It was years before I woke up with a start and realized I had inadvertently broken a rule. By that time the Baton Rouge Open was no longer a tournament. Once I realized my mistake there was nobody left to call. I didn't try to hide my error, but with the tournament defunct, and the prize money and trophy already awarded, I didn't know what to do. Later I learned that once a competition is closed, as this was clearly was, no further penalty can be incurred.

It was over forty years ago, but that one still bugs me. It was an honest mistake, but one I wish I had rectified.

Others have failed to replace their balls after causing them to move, some in more conspicuous circumstances than my error in Baton Rouge. In the 1997 Players Championship at the treacherous par-three 17th on Sunday, Davis Love III had successfully negotiated the water guarding all four sides of the green. That's usually the hard part. But as Love prepared to strike his birdie putt, he took a couple of practice strokes while looking at the hole as part of his normal pre-shot routine. Unfortunately, Love hit the ball with one of those practice strokes, sending it some five feet off to the side.

Embarrassed by what he'd done, Love properly assessed himself a one-stroke penalty, but he didn't replace the ball. He putted from the new spot, five feet away, and missed, thus giving him a four. But by not replacing the ball to its original position, Love should have added another penalty stroke. The score should have actually been a five. That mistake cost him more than one stroke. Love signed for the four, instead of the five on 17, and was disqualified for signing an incorrect card. He would have finished tied for seventh and made $105,000. Instead he went home having learned a valuable lesson.

The nuances of Rule 18 can cause great confusion, as Love found out in 1997. I made a mistake in 2001 by giving bad advice to my own partner concerning the same rule. It was during the Bay Hill Member-Guest, and my partner and close friend, Dick Ferris, chairman of the tour policy board, had a short putt on the 18th hole. We were playing aggregate scoring, which meant that all strokes from both players on a team counted. So when Ferris missed his short putt I winced. When he then knocked the ball off the green in disgust, my heart jumped into my throat.

"What are you doing?" I said. "You have to finish that."

"Oh, I forgot," Ferris said. One of the tournament rounds had been best ball, and he had forgotten the format for the day's play. "What do I do?"

"You have to go play it from the rough over there," I said.

"No," he said. "That can't be right."

"Yes," I insisted. "Now, get over there and finish this hole."

Not willing to argue the point any further with me, given how miffed I was, Ferris trudged off the rough, chipped back on, and two-putted for a quadruple bogey.

Days later, Ferris couldn't wait to see me when I arrived in my office at Bay Hill. "I knew I didn't have to play that shot," he

Dick Ferris, Clint Eastwood, Andy Bean, and I play a fair bit of golf together, but at the Bay Hill Member-Guest, I got a rule's lesson from Dick.
ARNOLD PALMER'S PERSONAL COLLECTION

said. "I called the USGA, and they said I had violated Rule 18-2. I should have penalized myself a shot and replaced the ball in its original position."

Sure enough, Ferris was right. While fit-pitching isn't specifically covered in the wording of Rule 18-2, it was the appropriate rule for Ferris's situation. I was wrong, but so was he. We should never have been in that position in the first place.

Ball in Motion
Deflected or Stopped

All sorts of things can alter the course and trajectory of a golf ball, and not many of them are good. In the professional game, we have galleries that often line the fairways and crowd behind the greens, and a lot of players have caught some pretty good breaks over the years by hitting fans, but there are as many bad bounces in those situations as good ones. Rule 19 deals with all situations in which a moving ball is deflected or stopped. The first part of the rule—**Rule 19-1**—reads:

> **If a ball in motion is accidentally deflected or stopped by any outside agency, it is a rub of the green, no penalty is incurred and the ball shall be played as it lies.**

Back in 1961 Gary Player caught a great break because of this rule. We were playing in the Masters, and back in those days, Cliff Roberts allowed spectators to come up very close to the right edge of the 15th green. He also allowed people to stand on the grass behind the 15th green between the fringe and the water. That was a great advantage as you were standing in the fairway of the par-five looking at a long second shot to a well-guarded green. The patrons behind the green were a great backstop. It almost made the water back there seem insignificant.

Gary thought so too, and in 1961 we were neck and neck through most of the back nine. Fifteen was the pivotal hole. Gary hit a great drive, and decided to go for it on his second shot. He hit a low cut shot that appeared to be headed for trouble, when suddenly a hand appeared out of the gallery and batted the ball back into play. Officials surrounded the patron and questioned his motives, but he claimed he was simply protecting himself, holding up his hand to keep the ball from hitting his head.

Whatever the cause, the spectator was an "outside agency" under Rule 19-1, and Gary played the ball where it lay without penalty. He went on to birdie the hole and win the Masters that year. I finished second. The next year, Mr. Roberts had rearranged the gallery ropes, pushing the crowds farther away from the right side of the 15th fairway and out from behind the green altogether.

Others who have had their balls deflected by outside agencies haven't been as fortunate. At the 2001 FleetBoston Classic, Tom Kite was one of those unfortunate souls. Kite was one shot behind Larry Nelson on Sunday afternoon with two holes to play. The closing holes, a par-three and a par-five, were both birdie

Tom Kite was none too pleased after his approach shot hit a bird in the 2001 FleetBoston Classic. ASSOCIATED PRESS/AP

opportunities, so Kite liked his chances. As he prepared to tee off on the 167-yard par-three 17th, Kite was thinking about a two.

The purple martin flying overhead never entered his mind. Kite's ball looked good for a couple of seconds. Then the martin swooped down and collided with the ball. Both the bird and the ball fell into the pond in front of the green.

"Talk about your all-time bad breaks," Nelson said. "You have to feel bad for Tom. He was playing really well."

Kite's ball had been deflected by an outside agency, and under Rule 18-1, he got no relief or dispensation for having hit a bird. His ball was in the hazard. Kite chipped onto the green and two-putted for a double bogey.

"The ball just fell out of the sky," Kite said. "I got myself in position to win the tournament and just came up a little bit short."

Sometimes Rule 19 calls for penalty strokes to be added when a ball in motion is deflected or stopped. According to the wording of Rule 19-2b:

> **If a competitor's ball is accidentally deflected or stopped by himself, his partner or either of their caddies or equipment, the competitor shall incur a penalty of two strokes. The ball shall be played as it lies, except when it comes to rest in or on the competitor's, his partner's or either of their caddie's clothes or equipment, in which case the competitor shall through the green or**

in a hazard drop the ball, or on the putting green place the ball, as near as possible to where the article was when the ball came to rest in or on it.

Leonard Thompson ran headfirst into this rule in the 1978 Quad Cities Open when his caddie tried to put a little body English on

Leonard Thompson's penalty for hitting his own equipment proved just how fickle the rules can sometimes be.
ASSOCIATED PRESS/AP

a putt that was headed for the hole. The exaggerated body language caused a tee to fall from behind the caddie's ear. The tee struck the ball, knocking it off line. Not only did Thompson miss what probably would have been a made birdie putt, he was assessed two shots because the ball was deflected by his own equipment.

Bob Murphy suffered a similar fate in the GTE Suncoast Classic at the TPC of Tampa Bay. Since joining the Senior PGA Tour, Murph has worn plantation hats that make him look like a Tennessee Williams character, and on the final round in Tampa the wide-brimmed chapeau cost Murphy a chance at victory.

Murph had hit his second shot on a par-five into a greenside bunker and was hoping to get up and down for birdie. Instead, the sand shot caught the lip of the bunker, then ricocheted backward and landed on the brim of Murph's hat. The result was a two-stroke penalty under Rule 18-2, and a triple-bogey eight on the hole.

There are times when officials have to apply their own judgment to situations, and even those when players are behaving badly. Such was the case in the 1999 U.S. Open in Pinehurst, North Carolina.

During Sunday's final round, John Daly, frustrated by the USGA's course setup, let his anger show on the 485-yard par-four eighth hole. After missing the green, Daly hit a pitch that didn't quite make it onto the putting surface. The ball began rolling back down the incline, but Daly had seen enough. He met the ball halfway down, and took a swipe at it with his putter, knocking the rolling ball off the front edge of the green.

John Daly's antics have gotten him into lots of trouble over the years, but the swipe he took at a moving ball in the 1999 U.S. Open could have easily resulted in a disqualification. ASSOCIATED PRESS/AP

It was a temper tantrum, pure and simple, and one that could have (and probably should have) cost Daly a disqualification. In order for Rule 19 to apply, the deflection of a moving ball has to be "accidental." There was nothing accidental or arbitrary about what Daly did. He was mad and disgusted, and he took a swipe at his ball in anger.

Ben Nelson, one of the more good-natured officials on the PGA Tour, took Daly's plight into consideration when meting out a penalty. Instead of disqualifying Daly on the spot, Nelson gave him a two-shot penalty for deflecting a moving ball. A kind gesture from a kind man, and probably better than Daly deserved.

Lifting, Dropping, Placing; Playing from a Wrong Place

If you've ever watched golf on television, you've probably seen Rule 20 in effect. A player is taking a drop from either an area where he gets free relief or an area where he is taking a penalty, and an official is standing watch over the proceedings. The official points to the area where the player may, in accordance with Rule 20, take a drop, and the player, following procedure to the letter, holds the ball shoulder high at arm's length and drops the ball in the prescribed spot.

Everybody watches the ball, eagerly anticipating the words that will make everything legal. If the drop is good and nothing more is required, the official will say, "That ball's in play." If things don't go exactly as they should, the official will step in again. If, for example, the dropped ball rolls closer to the hole, or rolls more than two club lengths, then the player will drop the ball again under the same procedures. If, after a third drop, the ball continues to roll into a bad place, the official will point (usually with the antenna of his walkie-talkie) to the spot where the ball hit the ground, and the player will place the ball on that spot. Then come the magic words from the official: "That ball's in play."

Players do their best to get all the procedures right, but they sometimes fail. P. H. Horgan III had finished his final round of the 1996 Nike Shreveport Open and was waiting by the 18th green for the last group to finish before heading back out for a playoff with Tim Loustalot. While waiting, Horgan struck up a conversation with the tournament director and relayed an incident that had occurred on Saturday.

It seemed that on the back nine of the third round, Horgan had accidentally dropped his ball on the green after having marked it, and the ball hit the marker, knocking it askew. Horgan replaced the mark and discussed it with his playing partner, and the two of them agreed there was no penalty. But the tournament director disagreed, citing **Rule 20-1**, which reads in part:

> **If a ball or ball-marker is accidentally moved in the process of lifting the ball under a Rule or marking its position, the ball or the ball-marker shall be replaced. There is no penalty provided the movement of the ball or the ball-marker is directly attributable to the specific act of marking the position of or lifting the ball. Otherwise,**

**the player shall incur a penalty stroke under this
Rule or Rule 18-2a.**

Horgan's accident had nothing to do with marking the ball. He
simply fumbled the ball, and it landed on his mark. The penalty

P. H. Horgan III learned a valuable lesson about marking
his ball while playing in the 1996 Nike Shreveport Open.
MICHAEL C. COHEN

should have been one stroke, but since Horgan didn't add that stroke to his Saturday scorecard, he was disqualified for signing a wrong card. Rather than entering the playoff for first, Horgan went home with a "disqualification" by his name.

Sometimes, even if a player gets all the dropping procedures right, he still screws up by dropping the ball in the wrong place. Sergio Garcia learned that lesson the hard way in the 2001 Greg Norman Holden International tournament. In the third round, while playing with Norman, the tournament host, Garcia hit his opening tee shot against a pinecone in the rough. He knew there was no relief from a pinecone, but players were entitled to relief from the large advertising billboards littered around the golf course. It's called "line of sight relief" from "temporary immovable obstructions," and you rarely ever see it used except at tour events where billboards, scoreboards, and grandstands are temporarily erected, but certainly immovable during the course of play. Garcia thought a billboard was in his line of sight. Norman agreed, and gave Garcia advice on where to drop.

Unfortunately for Garcia, the spot Norman suggested as the right one for the drop was about three feet away from the outside boundaries of his drop area. John Paramour, the chief rules official for the European PGA Tour, notified Garcia on the second hole that there might be a problem, and after the round, Paramour and Garcia went back to the spot. After a great deal of animated discussion, Paramour assessed Garcia with a two-stroke penalty under **Rule 20-7b**. The applicable rule reads in part:

If a competitor plays a stroke with his ball in play (i) which has been dropped or placed in a wrong place, or (ii) which has been moved and not replaced in a case where the Rules require replacement, he shall, provided a serious breach has not occurred, incur the penalty prescribed by the applicable Rule and play out the hole with the ball.

Paramour deemed Garcia's action to be without malice—he was simply acting on advice from the tournament host—and therefore the penalty was only two shots instead of disqualification.

"Thank god he wasn't disqualified," Norman said afterward. "According to John Paramour, if he had gone from a bad situation into a good situation and really improved his shot, it's disqualification. Under the interpretation I've had of that rule for years, Sergio did the right thing. I personally feel bad for him because he asked me for a ruling. From what I've learned today, ninety percent of golfers taking relief from those signs are violating the rules."

Garcia was perturbed. He was leading by two shots prior to the incident. After the third round, he was tied for the lead with Aaron Baddeley. He ultimately lost to Baddeley in a playoff, but by Sunday it was missed putts, not muffed drops that cost Garcia the title.

Sergio Garcia took what he thought was an appropriate drop during the Greg Norman Holden Invitational. He was especially confident in the procedure since he was playing with tournament host, Greg Norman. But officials saw things differently, and Garcia incurred a penalty. MATT TURNER/ALL SPORT

The Garcia incident wasn't the first time John Paramour had been called on to interpret a questionable drop and its implication under Rule 20-7b. A year before, at the 2000 Spanish Open at El Prat, Seve Ballesteros attempted to slice a ball around a tree from a hanging lie in the rough at the 11th hole. He pulled the shot out of bounds. After walking up to the 11th green and confirming that the ball was, indeed, out of play, Ballesteros returned to the original spot to drop another ball. He said he wasn't sure where the original spot was, so he asked the gallery (all of whom were great fans of Ballesteros). After picking the spot the fans had pointed out, Ballesteros dropped a ball and hit his fourth shot, but the tree was no longer in his line.

Television viewers who saw the incident immediately called in and cried foul. Paramour, the senior official on the scene, met with Ballesteros and walked through the incident, but, Paramour refused to review the television tapes, saying, "In my opinion, this is trial by television."

It was a question of fact whether or not Ballesteros took an improper drop, and the tapes confirmed that Ballesteros had played his fourth shot from a spot closer to the hole and in a better position than the original ball. If Paramour had ruled against Ballesteros, it would have been a two-shot penalty for violating Rule 20-7b. As it was, Paramour chose to rely on Ballesteros's word and the evidence from those on the scene at the time. He ruled that no penalty should be incurred.

Outraged television viewers accused Seve Ballesteros of cheating when he took a questionable drop in the 2000 Spanish Open. In that case, officials refused to view tapes of the incident to determine if the drop was legal.
ASSOCIATED PRESS/AP

More times than not, officials don't have to step in when players question themselves on drops. In my tournament, the Bay Hill Invitational, Jeff Sluman hit his ball in the hazard that fronts the par-three 17th green. Because we had a drop area lined off, Sluman played from that area and moved on. He shot a 69 that Friday and entered the weekend just two shots out of the lead.

Jeff Sluman wouldn't let the sun rise on an improper drop. After dropping in the wrong place during the Bay Hill Invitational, Sluman walked out the next morning with an official and righted things immediately. ASSOCIATED PRESS/AP

But later that night, the drop began to bother him. He knew the rule concerning drops from a hazard, and he thought he might have dropped his ball closer to the hole than the rules provide, even though he dropped in the drop zone.

Sluman walked out with an official the next morning and walked through the incident again. When the official concurred that he had probably played from a wrong spot, Sluman immediately disqualified himself. As far as he was concerned, it was the only honorable thing to do.

Cleaning Ball

In the old days, there was no need for Rule 21 because you didn't touch your ball from the moment you teed off on a hole until the ball fell in the cup. Any ball cleaning took place between holes. Irrigation changed that. Once courses were watered, balls picked up mud and made deep, penetrating indentations on the greens. The USGA and R&A found it necessary to write Rule 21 to allow players to clean their balls in certain situations. It reads in part:

> **A ball on the putting green may be cleaned when lifted under Rule 16-1b. Elsewhere, a ball may be cleaned when lifted except when it has been lifted:**
>
> **a. To determine if it is unfit for play (Rule 5-3);**
> **b. For identification (Rule 12-2), in which case**

**it may be cleaned only to the extent neces-
sary for identification; or**

**c. Because it is interfering with or assisting
play (Rule 22).**

**If a player cleans his ball during play of a hole
except as provided in this Rule, he shall incur a
penalty of one stroke and the ball, if lifted, shall
be replaced.**

Those who are serious about the rules of golf don't allow their personal feelings about a player or a situation to intrude on doing what's right when it comes to the rules. That was shown in the recent Curtis Cup Matches, the ladies' version of the Walker Cup Matches pitting American amateurs against their Great Britain and Ireland counterparts.

In the course of those matches, Mary Everard, a member of the British team, marked her ball at the request of her opponent, which is legal under the rules. What wasn't allowed was the good wiping Everard's caddie gave the ball with a towel. That was a violation of Rule 21.

The referee for the match, USGA administrator John Laupheimer, imposed a penalty of one stroke on Everard for improperly cleaning her ball. Everard accepted the penalty, and saved any unsavory comments she might have had for Laupheimer until the two of them got home. Laupheimer and Everard were husband and wife.

Ball Interfering With or Assisting Play

We used to have something called "stymies" in golf. If another player's ball was in the way of your ball, or, on the green, if another ball was in your line, you were "stymied." You either played around or over the other ball, since marking and lifting a ball was out of the question. Byron Nelson was a master at chipping his ball over another ball on the green, doing so with such deft touch that I often wondered if he wasn't better with a wedge on the greens than he was with a putter.

Once marking became an acceptable practice on the putting greens and elsewhere, **Rule 22** was put into effect. It says:

Any player may:

a. **Lift his ball if he considers that the ball might assist any other player or**
b. **Have any other ball lifted if he considers that the ball might interfere with his play or assist the play of any other player.**
c. **But this may not be done while another ball is in motion. In stroke play, a player required to lift his ball may play first rather than lift. A ball lifted under this Rule shall be replaced.**

I can't tell you the number of times I've had to mark my ball in the fairway or the rough so another player can play his shot. Usually it's not a big deal. I simply mark the ball with a tee or ball marker, and carefully lift it with two fingers so as not to inadvertently knock any mud or debris off the ball. The only time these marking procedures become a little testy is when both balls are in a bunker.

I've been in that situation as well. In a recent Senior PGA Tour event, my ball came to rest near another ball in the bunker. Under normal procedures as prescribed in Rule 22, I would mark my ball and allow the other player, who was away, to play first. But in this case, both our balls were in a footprint. I knew the rule, but I wanted to get clarification, so I called an official.

As it turned out my suspicions were correct. The official confirmed that I had to mark my ball, allow the other player to play, then restore the bunker to its original condition, which meant raking it, and adding the footprint back, as close in depth as possible, before placing my ball back in its original spot.

I think my foot was bigger than the guy's who left the print the first time, but I followed the rule and played out the hole. Sometimes it doesn't pay to hit the ball farther than your playing partner, even if it is only by a couple of inches.

Loose Impediments

Some of the most interesting and controversial rulings in golf center on Rule 23, and the definition of loose impediments. You've certainly read or heard about some of the more famous ones, but there are others that might have slipped under your radar. Every minute golf is played, somebody in the world is moving loose impediments, picking up pebbles, or flicking grass clippings aside. On tour players pick up leaves, sticks, mud clumps, and rocks all the time, cleaning as much debris as possible away from their balls.

All of which is perfectly legal under **Rule 23**. The rule defines "loose impediments" as:

> **Natural objects such as stones, leaves, twigs, branches and the like, dung, worms, and insects and casts or heaps made by them, provided they**

**are not fixed or growing, are not solidly embed-
ded and do not adhere to the ball.**

**Sand and loose soil are loose impediments on
the putting green but not elsewhere.**

**Snow and natural ice, other than frost, are
either casual water or loose impediments at the
option of the player.**

Manufactured ice is an obstruction.

Dew and frost are not loose impediments.

Under this **Rule 23-1**, players get relief from loose impediments,
not by moving their balls in any way, but by moving the impediments themselves. According to the rule:

**Except when both the loose impediment and
the ball lie in or touch the same hazard, any loose
impediment may be removed without penalty. If
the ball moves, see Rule 18-2c.**

**When a ball is in motion, a loose impediment
which might influence the movement of the ball
shall not be removed.**

For a few minutes in the 1999 State Farm Rail Classic, Janice
Moodie and the rules official following her group thought she
had violated Rule 23. Moodie, a tenacious Scot who has a won-

derful game and an equally pleasant disposition, trailed Korea's Mi Hyun Kim by a single shot in the final round when she hit her tee shot into a fairway bunker on the 13th hole. While taking her stance in the bunker, a butterfly landed on Moodie's ball. She backed away and shooed the insect away.

Enter the television rules police. Some viewer thought he had seen an infraction and called the tournament office. An insect is a "loose impediment," and since both Moodie's ball and the loose impediment were in the same hazard, the viewer claimed that shooing the bug away was a violation of Rule 23.

Angus Mackenzie, the LPGA official on site, agreed, and as Moodie finished the 15th, Mackenzie notified her that she needed to add two shots to her score for removing a loose impediment from a hazard. Rattled by the decision, Moodie bogeyed the 16th to seemingly drop from contention.

But Barb Trammell, the LPGA director of tournament operations, had been home watching the incident on television as well, and she didn't think the penalty was correct. Trammel called Tom Meeks of the USGA and confirmed her suspicions. The USGA and R&A had drafted a new decision on this very situation allowing a player to wave at an insect in a hazard to encourage its movement. In fact, a meeting was taking place in St. Andrews that very day to discuss a similar incident involving Fred Couples and a grasshopper at the 1996 President's Cup. I was captain of that team and remember the incident well. While standing in a bunker, Couples waved his hand over a grasshopper that had landed on his ball. There was a little discussion at the time, but no penalty was assessed. The dozen or so men meeting at the Royal and Ancient Golf Club in St. Andrews that afternoon had no idea what was happening in Springfield, Illinois, but they knew what Moodie and the LPGA officials on site didn't. What Moodie had done was completely legal under Rule 23. There should have been no penalty.

Trammell called Mackenzie and informed him that the penalty should be rescinded. Mackenzie hustled out to the 18th and caught Moodie on the tee, informing her that there had been a mistake. But by then it was too late. Moodie trailed by one after her bogey at 16. A birdie chip at the last hole came up inches short, and Moodie ended up tied for second, one shot behind Kim.

"I'm annoyed," Moodie said afterward. She was obviously disappointed, but she handled the situation with poise and grace. "I think it was handled poorly," was her only negative comment.

It seemed odd that in the same season one official thought shooing a butterfly was a violation of Rule 23, another saw nothing wrong with a dozen fans moving a 1,000-pound boulder away from a player's ball.

That's exactly what happened in Arizona at the 1999 Phoenix Open. In what is probably the most memorable (and certainly one of the most controversial) rulings of the last ten years, Tiger Woods got loose-impediment relief from a boulder that was bigger than most wrecking balls.

It happened on Sunday when Woods was paired with tournament leader Rocco Mediate in the final group of the day. On the par-five 13th at the TPC of Scottsdale, Woods hit his tee shot right of the fairway into a natural area, which in Phoenix means the desert. The ball came to rest behind a 1,000-pound boulder. Woods, having full knowledge of the rules, called PGA Tour official Orlando Pope over for a ruling. Was the boulder a loose impediment?

Pope said that since it was not imbedded, and it fit the technical definition, that the boulder was, indeed, considered a loose impediment and could be moved by the player, his caddie, his fellow competitor and his caddie, or any spectators who might want to lend a hand. Rocco and his caddie passed, but Woods had no trouble rounding up thirteen strong-backed youths from his gallery to push the stone out of the way.

Woods thanked the spectators, shook everyone's hand, then hit his second shot into the greenside bunker and got up-and-down for birdie.

"Tiger was very lucky there were a number of people in his gallery who were willing to move the rock for him," said tournament director Ben Nelson, himself a PGA Tour rules expert.

USGA manager of competitions Dave Donnelly said, "As far as the rules of golf go, a boulder is just a large stone and you're permitted to move it." Donnelly found himself saying that a lot in the days following Woods's boulder-moving incident. The phone calls and e-mails to the USGA after the event numbered in the thousands. But according to David Fay, executive director of the USGA, "The decisions book provided a real road map in this case. I commend Tiger for having the presence of mind to ask the right questions, and I'm not surprised the tour handled it without batting an eye."

Many of those who were upset by the ruling questioned the fairness of having gallery members move a rock for you. "What if that happens to me when nobody else is around?" Paul Azinger asked from the locker room shortly after the boulder was moved.

I personally don't think that should be a consideration. Galleries have always been an integral part of the professional game, and, for good and bad, some players are going to have more spectators than others. Sure, Woods gets an occasional break by having such large galleries. I did too when I was playing regularly. But Woods and I also get our share of bad breaks that are fan-related. How often has Azinger, or any other player for that matter, been stabbed by an overanxious autograph seeker with an ink pen? What about noise, and simply getting from a green to the next tee? How easy is it for Woods to go to the rest room at the golf course?

Tiger Woods got a little help from his friends in removing a loose impediment at the 1999 Phoenix Open. CRAIG JONES/ALL SPORT

Did Woods catch a good break by having enough people in his gallery willing to move a boulder out of his line? Sure he did. But, just like everything in golf, the good and bad even out at the end of the day. What Woods did in Phoenix was perfectly fair and legal under the rules. I commend him for knowing the rules well enough to ask.

Obstructions

According to the rule book definition, obstructions are:

Anything artificial, including the artificial surfaces and sides of roads and paths and manufactured ice, except:

a. **Objects defining out of bounds, such as walls, fences, stakes and railings;**
b. **Any part of an immovable artificial object which is out of bounds; and**
c. **Any construction declared by the Committee to be an integral part of the course.**

The rules also recognize that some obstructions, like soda cans, are movable, while others, like sprinkler heads and cart paths, are immovable. According to the definitions in the rule book:

> **An obstruction is a movable obstruction if it may be moved without unreasonable effort, without unduly delaying play and without causing damage. Otherwise it is an immovable obstruction.**

The differences between a loose impediment (Rule 23) and an obstruction can sometimes be confusing, and can cause problems for a player. The usual rule of thumb is if God made it, it's a loose impediment, and if man made it, it's an obstruction. But different tournaments on different continents make differing exceptions to the obstruction rule, as Nick Faldo found out during a trip to Indonesia.

It was the inaugural playing of the Alfred Dunhill Masters on the island of Bali, and Faldo was leading by six shots over Canadian Jack Kay going into the final round. It looked as though victory was certain, especially after Faldo got off to a strong start on Sunday. But on the 13th tee of the final round, officials informed Faldo that he had been disqualified for an incident from the previous day.

During the third round, Faldo's ball had come to rest next to a piece of coral lying in a bunker. If the coral was considered an obstruction, it would be a movable obstruction, and Faldo would be entitled to relief. **Rule 24-1** states in part:

A player may obtain relief from a movable obstruction as follows:

a. If the ball does not lie in or on the obstruction, the obstruction may be removed. If the
   ball moves, it shall be replaced, and there is
   no penalty provided that the movement of
   the ball is directly attributable to the
   removal of the obstruction. Otherwise, Rule
   18-2a applies.
b. If the ball lies in or on the obstruction, the
   ball may be lifted, without penalty, and the
   obstruction removed. The ball shall through
   the green or in a hazard be dropped, or on
   the putting green be placed, as near as possible to the spot directly under the place
   where the ball lay in or on the obstruction,
   but not nearer the hole.

There had been plenty of times in Faldo's career when he'd
taken relief from movable obstructions. At the Masters, he once
hit a ball on the par-five 15th that landed in a beer cup. Under
Rule 24, he lifted the ball, moved the cup, and dropped the ball as
near as possible to the original spot. It was no big deal. It happened all the time on tour.

Faldo thought nothing about removing the coral. Even
though coral is not artificial, European Tour rules allowed such
items to be removed from hazards, a local provision to Rule 24.

But the Alfred Dunhill Masters was part of the Australasian PGA Tour, which did not have such a local rule. Under the Australasian interpretation of Rule 24, Faldo had not removed a movable obstruction from the hazard, he had lifted a natural object, a "loose impediment" from a hazard, which is a violation of the rules.

New Zealand's Michael Campbell saw the incident and was sure Faldo had breached the rule. He reported it to Australasian PGA Tour chief Brian Allan, who gave Faldo the bad news. He had broken the rules on Saturday, failed to assess himself the necessary penalty, signed an incorrect scorecard, and was, therefore, disqualified.

"I just wasn't thinking," Faldo said. "This was the first time I've been disqualified a day after the event."

Kay went on to win the first Alfred Dunhill Masters, but even he felt bad for Faldo. "We all know who really won the tournament," Kay said afterward. "As far as I'm concerned, I finished second and received first-place money. I have never played in Europe, though, so I would never dream of touching anything in a bunker."

The tournament was moved to Jakarta the following year, but Faldo didn't return. About the only thing good that came from this unfortunate incident was the formation of a World Forum of PGA Tours. According to Allan, "This incident was the catalyst for addressing the issue of uniformity in playing conditions on the world's major tours."

As the design of golf courses change, obstruction rulings will continue to become more frequent and more complex. In the old days obstructions were few and far between. You might occasionally get relief from a trash can or a halfway house, but little else. Today, with wall-to-wall cart paths on almost every golf course, sprinkler heads everywhere, and all sorts of rock walls and other man-made features littering courses, the need for rulings has become prevalent.

I believe we need to go back to some of the older standards for relief. For example, one of the best holes in the world is the par-four 17th on the Old Course at St. Andrews, Scotland, one of the oldest golf courses in the world. The Old Course's most famous hole is the 475-yard par-four, known as the Road Hole. The fairway and green are bordered on the right by a gravel road, which is bordered on one side by an ancient stone wall. If the old course were built today, these features would be deemed "obstructions" and players would have little trouble firing their approaches into the narrow green. If your ball flew over the green, it would be no problem. You'd simply take relief from the road and play away.

But the road that borders it is an integral part of the golf course, making the strategy of the hole particularly challenging. I've seen plenty of players overshoot the 17th green and find themselves against the stone wall. Their only option at that point is to try to ricochet their shots off the wall back onto the green. Because the consequences of overshooting the 17th are so severe, a lot of players bail out of the left and leave themselves with difficult pitch shots to the narrow green.

In 1960, when I played in the Open Championship for the first time at St. Andrews, I got a taste of just how difficult the 17th can play. When I reached that hole, I had cut Kel Nagle's lead in the championship to one shot and I felt the tournament was mine to win. I had always played aggressively, especially when I found myself close to the lead in the final moments of a championship, and this was no exception. If I could close with a couple of birdies, I had a better-than-average chance of winning the first Open Championship I ever played in.

I had played the 17th conservatively all week, and it had cost me. Although I had reached the narrow green in regulation, I had three-putted the thing three times. This was, in part, because of the way I played my approaches. I couldn't fly the ball right at the flag because going over the green was a sure-fire bogey or worse. The road was less than three feet from the edge of the green, and the wall abutted the opposite side of the road. To hit the ball long meant having to negotiate those obstacles (obstructions, in today's vernacular), which was no bargain. I played to the left side of the green every day and it cost me.

In the final round, I knew I needed a birdie so I played right at the flag. Unfortunately, I was so pumped up by being in contention I flew the ball long, and it ended up on the road. Pitch shots off gravel roads are not the kinds of shots you practice every day, so I had to be creative. Fortunately the ball had stopped in the middle of the road, and the wall didn't come into play. I chose to run the ball up the little bank separating the road from the green, and it worked. I hit perhaps the best recovery shot of the week, rolling the ball close enough to sink my par putt with relative ease.

But it was too little too late. Nagle parred the final two holes and won the Open by a shot, and the 17th, the hole with the obstructions that aren't, cost me my first British title.

The Old Course at St. Andrews is one of my favorite golf courses in the world, even though I've had more than my fair share of troubles with the road at the 17th. ARNOLD PALMER'S PERSONAL COLLECTION

Fourteen years after my run-in with the Road Hole in my Open debut, Gary Player had his own Open Championship challenge at the 1974 tournament at Royal Lytham and St. Annes. Leading through the final round, Gary bogeyed the 17th, but came to the final hole needing only a bogey or better to capture his third Open Championship title. He pushed his tee shot in the high rough, and, with a thrashing swing, he sent his second shot over the green and against the clubhouse.

The old brick clubhouse is only four paces off the green, and it comes into play regularly. By today's standards, unless denoted out of bounds, the clubhouse would be an obstruction. But the

R&A did, and still does, consider the clubhouse an integral part of the golf course. Gary had hit his ball there, and he would either have to play it or take a penalty stroke.

After much deliberation, Gary turned to his caddie and said, "Rabbit, can we win from here?"

"Mr. Gary," Rabbit said, "Ray Charles could win from here."

On that encouraging note, Gary turned his putter upside down and hit a left-handed punch shot. The ball popped up in the air and stopped ten feet from the hole. Gary two-putted and won by four shots over Peter Oosterhuis and Jack Nicklaus. Afterward Gary kissed his putter before kissing the Claret Jug.

Gary Player was pleased with his creative finish at Royal Lytham and St. Annes in the 1974 British Open. ASSOCIATED PRESS/AP

On the PGA Tour, such situations are almost never seen. We get relief from sprinkler boxes, even if they're thirty yards deep in the woods, and we get something called "line of sight" relief if a television tower or grandstand happens to be in our line. In the 2001 WGC-NEC Invitational at Firestone Country Club, Tiger Woods hooked his tee shot on the 18th hole into a terrible position. But rather than having to play the shot, Woods called over an official. The two of them looked at the line of the shot, and the official agreed to give Woods a free drop.

What was the ruling? A couple of cables holding up a scoreboard were on Woods's line to the hole. Never mind that in order

Temporary immovable obstructions (or TIOs as rules officials call them) create all sorts of questionable rulings, like the drop Tiger Woods got from a scoreboard cable during the 2001 WGC-NEC Invitational. ASSOCIATED PRESS/AP

to hit those cables Woods would have had to hit a low screaming shot that had no chance of reaching the green. The very fact that the cables were in his "line of sight" was enough to get a drop.

It's not just players and spectators who get confused by the obstruction rules. Sometimes officials get it wrong. In the first hole of the final round of the 1994 U.S. Open, Dr. Trey Holland, the rules official for Ernie Els's group, had to make a ruling right off the bat. After pushing his tee shot, Els had a television camera crane right on his line. He asked Holland for a ruling, and

Ernie Els couldn't have been happier after receiving a favorable (and wrong) ruling from Trey Holland in the 1994 U.S. Open. Els went on to win the championship in a playoff. ASSOCIATED PRESS/AP

Holland said the crane was a temporary immovable obstruction and Els was entitled to relief.

Els took relief, bogeyed the hole, and went on to win that U.S. Open in a three-way playoff the next day. Holland, however, had to face the fact that he had made an erroneous ruling. The camera vehicle was temporary, but it was very movable. In fact it had four wheels, a motor, and a driver sitting nearby. The only thing you had to do to move it was turn a key. Holland hadn't checked out the crane before making his ruling, and he made a bad call, giving Els a drop he wasn't entitled to receive.

"I feel bad about it," Holland said many years later. "This is not a rationalization or an excuse, but I'd like to think it didn't make any difference in the outcome. It was a mistake and I feel bad about it."

Without the vagaries that are inherent in Rule 24, there would have never been a question. Holland would have told Els to play on, and that would have been the end of it. As it stands, Els still must answer questions about the favorable ruling he received, and Holland must continue to take the heat for giving inappropriate relief in a major championship to the ultimate winner.

No discussions are pending concerning a change in Rule 24. In 2000, Trey Holland became president of the USGA.

Abnormal
Ground Conditions

Most people know that you get a drop from casual water, but a lot of folks have no idea how to define *casual water* or other abnormal ground conditions. According to the rule book's definition:

> **An "abnormal ground condition" is any casual water, ground under repair or hole, cast or runway on the course made by a burrowing animal, a reptile or a bird.**

A burrrowing animal is defined as:

...An animal that makes a hole for habitation or shelter, such as a rabbit, mole, ground hog, gopher or salamander.

In recent years fire ants have been added to the list, even though garden variety black ants don't qualify. The logic of that ruling is that fire ants present a danger to the golfer standing on or near the anthill, while black ants are merely an annoyance. I don't know many entomologists on the PGA Tour, and I've never played with anyone who has read Edward O. Wilson's trilogy, *The Insect Societies,* but if you want to take relief from an anthill as an unnatural ground condition created by a burrowing animal, it's best to know your genus and species.

The most common abnormal ground conditions are ground under repair and casual water. Players get relief from these unusual conditions when:

A ball lies in or touches the condition or when such a condition interferes with the player's stance or the area of his intended swing. If the player's ball lies on the putting green, interference also occurs if such condition on the putting green intervenes on his line of putt. Otherwise, intervention on the line of play is not, of itself, interference under this Rule.

If the player finds his ball in such a condition, relief is granted under the rules. That relief takes place as follows:

Except when the ball is in a water hazard or a lateral water hazard, a player may obtain relief from interference by an abnormal ground condition as follows:

(i) Through the Green: If the ball lies through the green, the nearest point of relief shall be determined which is not in a hazard or on a putting green. The player shall lift the ball and drop it without penalty within one club-length of and not nearer the hole than the nearest point of relief, on part of the course which avoids interference (as defined) by the condition and is not in a hazard or on a putting green.

(ii) In a Bunker: If the ball is in a bunker, the player shall lift and drop the ball either:

(a) Without penalty in accordance with Clause (i) above, except that the nearest point of relief must be in the bunker and the ball must be dropped in the bunker, or if complete relief is impossible, in the bunker as near as possible to the spot where the ball lay, but not nearer the

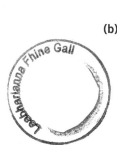

        hole, on a part of the course which affords maximum available relief from the condition; or

(b) Under penalty of one stroke, outside the bunker keeping the point where the ball lay directly between the hole and the spot on which the ball is dropped, with no limit to how far behind the bunker the ball may be dropped.

This rule actually led to the cancellation of a PGA Tour event in what still ranks as one of the most hotly debated decisions in tour history.

It was early February of 1996, and, as is usually the case along the Monterey Peninsula that time of year, it rained like water pouring from a boot. I can't remember a year when we had more rain in that part of California, and I've been playing out there for over forty years. The 1996 season was particularly bad because the rain had been a nonstop occurrence for most of the winter, leaving little room for any additional water as the AT&T Pebble Beach National Pro-Am (formerly the Bing Crosby Clambake) rolled around.

According to David Eger, who was the tournament director that year, "Poppy Hills and Spyglass were saturated, and there was simply nowhere else for the water to go. There had been three or four days of dry weather, which allowed us to start the golf tournament, but we had to play lift-clean-and-place. On Friday it started raining, and there were several holes at Poppy Hills that were unplayable. Saturday we couldn't play and the forecast wasn't much better. On Sunday it rained more. One hole at Spyglass was still unplayable, because in order to take full relief from casual water you had to go all the way into the woods. Even though we were playing lift-clean-and-place, there were places where you couldn't take relief and get out of two inches of water. The forecast called for more rain on Monday, and that's when we decided to call it off."

They certainly could have played, but it would have required some decisions on relief from casual water that would have been unpopular. As Eger put it, "Suppose the guy leading the golf tournament said he couldn't find relief. Were we going to make him drop his ball in the woods?"

According to Rule 25, that's the only option Eger and the tour had. The only situation in which a player can take partial relief from casual water is when the ball is in a bunker. Otherwise, relief means full relief. And in the case of Pebble Beach and some of its surrounding courses, that can mean going all the way to Palo Alto. The decision to cancel the 1996 AT&T Pebble Beach National Pro-Am was the only logical decision tour officials could make under the circumstances. The heat Eger took for the decision was unwarranted. He did the only thing he could, given the hand dealt to him by Mother Nature and Rule 25.

The good news for golfers playing in sloppy casual water conditions is that, under Rule 25, a ball lost in casual water or a burrowing animal hole is not considered a lost ball. Instead it's considered a ball lost in "unusual ground," and the player can take a drop without penalty.

I would have thought Tom Watson, a man who has always prided himself on his knowledge of the rules, would have known that and taken advantage of it when his ball plugged in casual water and was lost in my tournament, the Bay Hill Invitational. Watson searched for his ball in a low-lying area that wasn't marked as a hazard, but where standing water was prevalent. Under Rule 25, he should have been able to take relief. The rule reads in part:

> **It is a question of fact whether a ball lost after having been struck toward an abnormal ground condition is lost in such condition. In order to treat the ball as lost in the abnormal ground condition, there must be reasonable evidence to that effect. In the absence of such evidence, the ball must be treated as a lost ball and Rule 27 applies.**
>
> **If a ball is lost in an abnormal ground condition, the spot where the ball last entered the condition shall be determined and, for the purposes of applying this Rule, the ball shall be deemed to lie at this spot.**
>
> **If the ball last entered the abnormal ground condition at a spot through the green, the player may substitute another ball without penalty and take relief as prescribed in Rule 25-1b(i).**

Tom Watson should have known that you can't lose a ball in casual water, but at my tournament, the Bay Hill Invitational, Watson took a penalty he didn't deserve. MICHAEL C. COHEN

No one disputed the fact that Watson's ball was lost in casual water. There was ample evidence, including eyewitnesses, to support that position. But Watson didn't take advantage of his fortune. Instead he declared the ball to be lost and trotted back to the tee to hit another ball. Once he struck the tee shot a second time, that new ball became the ball in play and the fact that he could have taken free relief much closer was negated.

"Oh, well," was about all Watson could say afterward. "I guess I cost myself a couple of shots."

Water Hazards, Including Lateral Water Hazards

Water hazards and lateral water hazards can be tricky because they encompass so many different bodies of water and conditions of play. By definition, a water hazard is:

> ...Any sea, lake, pond, river, ditch, surface drainage ditch or other open water course (whether or not containing water) and anything of a similar nature....

That can range from the drainage ditch behind one of your par-threes, to the Pacific Ocean, as I found out twice in two of the most memorable water hazard incidents in my career, both of which I would just as soon forget.

Oddly enough, both incidents occurred on the same hole, the beautiful 17th at Pebble Beach. In 1963, in the third round of the Crosby (which was the common name for what is now the AT&T Pebble Beach Pro-Am), I hit a ball over the green and apparently into the ocean. I wasn't sure how you played the ocean, so I decided to hit a provisional ball in case my original ball could not be found or played. I did this to speed up play. If my original ball was found, I assumed I could simply abandon my provisional ball and play on. If the original ball could not be found, I could play the provisional ball under penalty of stroke and distance.

There was only one problem: You can't play a provisional ball when your original ball might be in a water hazard. The ocean, it turned out, was played as a hazard, and the moment I struck that second ball from the tee, I had, in effect, abandoned my original ball. Not knowing the rule was no excuse, and when I found and played my original ball in the rocks behind the green, I had, in effect, played a wrong ball.

Two days later while I was sitting in the clubhouse, a rules official broke the bad news. I was disqualified for signing an incorrect scorecard, as I had played a wrong ball on the 17th hole without adding the appropriate penalty and correcting the mistake.

That disqualification ended a streak of forty-seven consecutive weeks I'd been in the money on tour. From that moment forward, I always checked the status of any area before I proceeded to hit a provisional ball.

Had I known that this was technically a "wrong ball," I would have never ventured down to hit it. ASSOCIATED PRESS/AP

A year later, on the same hole, I had another disaster. This time, however, I wasn't disqualified, although I might as well have been. It was the third round again, and, once again, I hit my shot on 17 over the green and into the rocks separating the golf course from the ocean. This time, rather than hitting a provisional ball as I had the year before, I walked down onto the rocks and found my ball.

I felt sure I could play the ball from there, so I took out my wedge and swung away. When the ball failed to exit the rocks, and ended up in a tougher spot than the one I had originally, I found myself in a curious position. If I wanted to take relief, I would either have to drop the ball back in its original position, or take it out to the spot where I last played a shot from outside the hazard, or, keeping the ball on a line with the hole, take it backward. The exact wording of my options is:

If a ball is in or is lost in a water hazard (whether the ball lies in water or not) the player may under penalty of one stroke:

a. Play a ball as nearly as possible at the spot from which the original ball was last played (see Rule 20-5); or

b. Drop a ball behind the water hazard, keeping the point at which the original ball last crossed the margin of the water hazard directly between the hole and the spot on which the ball is dropped, with no limit to how far behind the water hazard the ball may be dropped.

As commentator Jimmy Demaret quipped at the time, "His nearest drop under the rules would be in Honolulu." But I didn't exercise any of my drop options. Instead I stayed with it, swinging away in that hazard for more than twenty minutes with my gallery, three spectators, a rules official, my caddie, and a stray dog that had wandered down onto the rocks, staring at me curiously. I took a nine on the hole.

I've had a lot of miserable moments in golf, but hacking it around on the rocks during the 1964 Crosby Clambake was certainly one of the worst.
ASSOCIATED PRESS/AP

By the time I got into the clubhouse after my fiasco, the bartender at Pebble Beach had invented a new drink, which he offered me. "What do you call it?" I asked.

"Palmer on the Rocks," he deadpanned.

I didn't care for it then, and I still don't today.

Ball Lost or
Out of Bounds

It shouldn't be too difficult to define a lost ball. If you can't find your ball it's lost, right? The answer is, "not exactly." According to the definition of "lost ball," a ball is "lost" if:

a. It is not found or identified as his by the player within five minutes after the player's side or his or their caddies have begun to search for it; or

b. The player has put another ball into play under the Rules, even though he may not have searched for the original ball; or

c. The player has played any stroke with a provisional ball from the place where the original ball is likely to be or from a point nearer

the hole than that place, whereupon the provisional ball becomes the ball in play.

That seems like a lot of words to state the obvious. At first glance it looks as though the USGA and R&A could have saved a lot of ink and paper by simply saying "a lost ball is a ball you can't find." But the provisions of the "lost ball" definition are critical to keeping play moving and keeping standards consistent. Without a standard definition, some players would send out all-night search parties for their balls, and play would come to a screeching halt.

To set reasonable parameters the USGA and R&A have stated that five minutes is the maximum amount of time you can spend hunting for a golf ball. If it is found and identified during that five-minute period, you don't have to take a "lost ball" penalty. If it's found ten minutes later, too bad: The ball is deemed to be "lost" even though you have it in your hand.

Nobody needs to explain that rule to Greg Norman, a man who has taken it on the chin more often at the Masters than any other player in history. When I first saw Greg play Augusta National, I was certain he would win the Masters more than once. His game seemed perfect for the course, and for the better part of a decade, he was the number one player in the world. But time and time again, Greg walked away from Augusta having found nothing but heartbreak and disappointment.

The 1999 Masters was one such disappointment. When Greg played himself into contention on Friday, he became the crowd favorite. Everyone wanted to see him win the one tournament that had eluded him so many times. The Augusta faithful clearly took Greg's side.

Then on Saturday at the treacherous par-three 12th—the same hole where I had my plugged-ball controversy during my first Masters win—Greg hit what he thought was a perfect 8-iron shot. He was stunned when the ball flew over the bunkers and disappeared into the wiry brush that covers the hill behind that green. And he was even more stunned when he couldn't find his ball.

"I thought, 'This is the Masters. How can you possibly lose a ball?'" Greg said.

But that's exactly what happened. Greg and his caddie, along with his playing partner Lee Janzen, Lee's caddie, and two Masters

Hard to believe you can lose a ball at Augusta National, but as Greg Norman found out in 1999, anything's possible. DAVID CANNON/ALL SPORT

officials, combed the area for a full four minutes. Then Greg started his march back to the tee while the other four men continued the search to no avail. After five minutes, Greg's ball was deemed to be lost, and he played another shot from the tee, having taken a one-stroke penalty.

To his credit, Greg hit a tremendous second tee shot, flying the ball twenty feet behind the hole, then rolling the putt in for what was, perhaps, the best bogey of the entire tournament.

Later that afternoon, CBS announcer Bobby Clampett went back to the scene and found Greg's original ball some eight feet from where the five men had searched so desperately. Had Greg been given another five or ten minutes, someone would have surely found the original ball. But Rule 27 is clear on this point. Even if the ball had been found in the sixth minute, it was too late. Greg's ball was lost.

In theory Rule 27 should work consistently for every player, but unfortunately that's not always the case. Even in major championships, players, caddies, and most officials don't carry stopwatches, so when a search begins it isn't often that someone times the process to the exact second.

Mark O'Meara found that out during the 1998 Open Championship at Royal Birkdale. The Open Championship is always contested under windy and chilly conditions, but Saturday's third round in Southport, England, was particularly brutal, even by British standards. Winds topped forty knots by the afternoon and twenty-three of the eighty-one players who made the cut failed to break 80 on Saturday. Nobody broke par.

It was no wonder that there were more than a few errant shots that resulted in balls almost being lost. Lost balls are not common on tour, primarily because we have galleries. At the Open Championship, as many as 75,000 people per day pour onto the grounds to watch. It hard to imagine losing a ball with that many eyewitnesses nearby.

But that's what almost happened to O'Meara. On the sixth hole at Birkdale, O'Meara lost his tee shot to the right, and it landed in waist-high grass. After a three-minute search, O'Meara started back to the tee, at which point one of the Open patrons found the ball and unwittingly picked it up. O'Meara was summoned back to identify the ball.

Two questions arose from this incident: First, could a spectator engage in the search for a lost ball under the rules? And secondly, did O'Meara return to identify his ball within the five-minute time frame?

The answer to the first question was "yes." Anyone can help a player locate his ball, but only the player can identify the ball as being his. That brings up the second question: Did O'Meara get back in time?

"There was a lot of miscommunication," O'Meara said. "The USGA was on the phone; the R&A was on the phone. It was like Watergate out there. Nobody would make the call."

The official on the scene eventually ruled that O'Meara had, indeed, returned to identify his ball within the allotted time under the rules. At that point the matter was over. O'Meara took a drop (since the unsuspecting spectator had picked up the ball) and he went on to make par en route to winning the 1998 Open Championship.

A lot of people thought Mark O'Meara caught a break when his seemingly lost ball was found during the 1998 British Open, but it was O'Meara's good play that made him the champion. MICHAEL C. COHEN

A lot of people still debate whether or not O'Meara got a break, but the point is moot. The official on the scene made the ruling, and that was that. Had there been no official, it would have been up to Mark and his fellow competitors to make the call on their own. I have no doubt that they would have done the right thing.

Since balls don't get lost very often, the need for provisional balls isn't as prevalent on tour as, say, during the Saturday fourball match at your local club. Still, touring professionals do play provisional balls when they think their original balls might be lost or out of bounds.

A provisional ball is simply a second ball that is played "just in case" the original ball is out of play. If the original ball is found, under the rules, players forget about the provisional and play the original ball. If the original ball is, indeed, lost or out of bounds, the provisional ball becomes the ball in play and the appropriate penalty strokes are added.

But if you walk past the spot where your original ball might be (whether it's in a bush or close to an out-of-bounds stake) and play your provisional ball from a spot closer to the hole than the original ball, your original ball is deemed to be lost, even if it's in plain view.

Australian Stephen Leaney was faced with an interesting twist to this rule in the 2000 Alfred Dunhill Cup at the Old Course at St. Andrews. Playing with John Daly, Leaney snap-hooked his tee shot on the par-four 12th in a gorse bush. The ball was most likely lost, but even if it was found Leaney probably couldn't play it. Before leaving the 12th tee Leaney hit a provisional ball and drove it onto the green, leaving himself little more than a six-footer for par.

As they walked off the tee, Daly proceeded toward the bush to search for Leaney's original ball. Leaney didn't want anyone finding the original. He wanted his provisional ball to become the ball in play.

David Garland, the tournament official on the scene, informed Leaney that if he hustled up to the green and putted his provisional ball before anyone found the original, the provisional ball would automatically become the ball in play, and any further search for the first ball would be meaningless. The first ball would be deemed "lost" under the rules.

"But what about playing out of turn?" Leaney asked. Daly was

The incident could have prompted a footrace to the 13th green, but Stephen Leaney and John Daly worked out their rules questions like gentlemen during the 2000 Alfred Dunhill Cup. ASSOCIATED PRESS/AP

away, and if Leaney trotted up to the green and putted, he would be playing out of turn.

Garland informed Leaney that if the Dunhill Cup were a match play competition Daly could demand that the shot be canceled, and Leaney would have to replay the shot in the right order (Rule 10-1c), but because this was a stroke play event there would be no penalty for playing out of turn.

Two minutes later the point was moot. Daly realized that Leaney had no intention of looking for his original ball, and he quickly called off the search, thus avoiding what could have been an awkward footrace down the 12th fairway.

"John was very sporting about it," Leaney said. "If I had been forced to take an unplayable lie from the bush, I could have taken a five or a six."

As it was, Leaney made his six-foot putt for a par four and went on to shoot five-under-par 67 for the day.

I've hit more than my share of balls out of bounds or into areas where they couldn't be found over my career, but none as memorable as the two back-to-back shots I hit out of bounds on the 14th hole at Pebble Beach in the 1967 Crosby. At the time I trailed Jack Nicklaus by a single shot, when my first ball hit a tree that extended out into play. The ball careened off the tree and landed out of bounds. In accordance with Rule 27, I played my next shot from the same spot as my first, having taken a stroke and distance penalty, but that shot also caught the same tree, ricocheted in the same direction, and landed out of bounds only a few feet from my first ball. I took a nine on the hole and finished third in the tournament behind Nicklaus and Billy Casper.

That night a storm blew through Monterey and uprooted the tree, blowing it to the ground. Unfortunately, it was one day and five shots too late.

Ball Unplayable

Sometimes finding the ball is just as bad, if not worse, than losing it. I know I've hit some shots into places where I didn't want
to find it, and plenty of other players have done the same thing.

One of them was Phil Mickelson at the 2001 Buick Invitational at Torrey Pines near San Diego. Tied at the end of regulation with Davis Love III and Frank Lickliter, Mickelson trotted
back out to the 16th hole for a sudden death playoff. Love was
eliminated on the 16th when he made bogey, so Mickelson and
Lickliter continued to the par-four 17th a short hole dogleg left
with a canyon guarding the left side of the fairway.

Mickelson, the first to play on the 17th, hit his worst tee shot
of the day, pushing a driver into the canyon where there was
nothing but scrub bushes and rocks on a huge embankment leading down to the ocean. All Lickliter needed to do was find the
fairway and the advantage would swing in his favor.

Inexplicably, Lickliter hit a driver instead of playing safe with
an iron. He also hit one of the worst drives of his round, a rope

hook that landed in almost the same spot as Mickelson's ball. Both players hit provisional balls, assuming their original balls would not be found, and both provisional balls were safely in the fairway.

As they walked off the tee, Mickelson noticed several volunteer marshals trudging down the hillside to search for the balls. He began shouting, "Don't go down there!" and "Leave it!" With his provisional ball safely in play, Mickelson did not want the original ball to be found.

Unfortunately his calls went unheeded, and the original ball was found in a bush. Angry that his pleads had been ignored, Mickelson asked for a ruling. It was as he expected. According to PGA Tour rules official Mark Russell, "Once that ball was found, he was obligated to identify it as his."

Mickelson didn't want to go into the canyon. "If you find the original ball, the provisional is no good," he said, and he was right. Once the original ball was found, it became the ball in play, and the provisional, no matter how good it might be, had to be abandoned.

"I had asked the gentleman to please stop looking for the ball," Mickelson said. "He found one, and it happened to be mine. He was trying to do his job. I just wished that he hadn't done it so effectively."

The ball in the bush did, indeed, belong to Mickelson. At that point, playing the original ball was out of the question. Even if he had a swing, there was nowhere to go. He was thirty feet below the level of the fairway with nowhere to stand and no shot to play. At that point he had to declare his ball "unplayable." **Rule 28** states in part:

Under penalty of one stroke:

a. Play a ball as nearly as possible at the spot from which the original ball was last played (see Rule 20-5); or

b. Drop a ball within two club-lengths of the spot where the ball lay, but not nearer the hole; or

c. Drop a ball behind the point where the ball lay, keeping that point directly between the hole and the spot on which the ball is dropped, with no limit to how far behind that point the ball may be dropped.

The two-club-length-option was no good. Two club lengths from the bush was still in the bush, still in the canyon, and still unplayable. He also couldn't keep the point of the original ball directly between the hole and the spot where a ball could be dropped, because that would move him either farther down the canyon or into the Pacific. Mickelson's only option was to go back to the tee and play another ball, his fourth shot from that tee (counting his play of the 17th in regulation) in the course of an hour.

Mickelson hung around in the canyon for a few seconds more, seeing if Lickliter's ball was also found. It was, and the same options applied. Both players went back to the tee. Lickliter hit his second ball into the fairway, but Mickelson pushed another one. This time the tee shot hit a tree and bounced out of the canyon and into the rough. From there Mickelson hit his fourth shot to within twenty-five feet and two-putted for double bogey. That turned out to be enough, as Lickliter took three shots to get down from twenty feet for triple bogey, seven.

It was an ugly way to win, as Mickelson later admitted, but it was a win nonetheless.

Other Forms of Play

There are all kinds of games other than the traditional one-on-one match play or every-man-for-himself stroke play competitions you regularly see played at the professional level. Rules 29 through 34 outline those rules and go through what each means. You've got games like threesomes, in which one player plays his own ball in a match against two other people playing alternate shot, and foursomes, in which two players play against two other players in alternate shot with each team playing only one ball. The only time you see foursomes played on television these days are in the biannual Ryder Cup, President's Cup, and Solheim Cup matches, and in the World Cup of Golf, a WGC event in which two-man teams from around the world compete against each other in a stroke play competition.

Even then the format is not without controversy. Peter Thomson, captain of the International Team that played the Americans in the 2000 President's Cup, called foursomes "a bloody English invention for little old ladies to play at their clubs." While meant in good fun, that description was a little harsh, but lots of players agreed with him.

"Alternate shot or 'foursomes' is not a game you play very often, and it's a game that is almost never played at clubs around the world," Davis Love said. "It's hard to follow, and it's hard to play. Most people don't understand it."

Executives at Titleist certainly didn't understand it in December of 2000 when Tiger Woods and David Duval played together in the World Cup of Golf in Buenos Aires, Argentina. The folks at Titleist were already a little edgy about Duval. While designers at Footjoy (a sister company to Titleist) were designing a

Alternate Shot (or Foursomes) got David Duval into some hot water with one of his sponsors, but he and Tiger Woods ended up winning the 2000 World Cup of Golf anyway. ASSOCIATED PRESS/AP

shoe that didn't hurt his feet, they agreed to let Duval wear Nike golf shoes, even though he was contracted with Titleist and Footjoy. Some of the top brass in New Bedford, Massachusetts, didn't like the idea of their star wearing a competitor's product. When Duval was seen playing a Nike ball in Argentina, Titleist threatened to sue for breach of contract.

What they didn't realize at the time was that Duval was playing a Nike ball because his partner, Tiger Woods, played Nike balls. In alternate shot (or foursomes) the team would only play one ball. Woods was the best player in the world, so he got to choose which brand of ball the team played. Duval needed to get

Peter Thomson had some great one-liners during the 2000 President's Cup Matches, but none better than his quip about Foursomes being, "a bloody English invention." HARRY HOW/ALL SPORT

accustomed to playing that ball, so he played it throughout the matches in Buenos Aires.

Duval and Woods won the World Cup of Golf, and Titleist did, indeed, sue Duval for breach of contract, all because of a silly English game for ladies to play at their clubs on Sundays.

The group that decides what the format will be and what rules will apply is called the Committee, and they are the ultimate arbiters of what goes on inside the ropes at a competition. If a Committeeman makes a bad ruling, the ruling stands (as evidenced by many of the examples in this book). They decide how long the contest will be, what the course setup will be, how ties will be decided, and under which format the tournament will be played.

They have the ability to interpret disputed procedures and find questions of fact, and, in some instances, bend a rule or two. In the 2002 Ryder Cup Matches, for example, captains Curtis Strange and Sam Torrence agreed ahead of time that, in the interest of speeding up the matches, they would not allow any practice putting or chipping during the matches. According to the rules, players may practice putting on the hole they've just completed as long as such practice does not unduly delay play.

On the surface it looked as if Strange and Torrence had broken Rule 1 by agreeing to break a rule. But their out was the "unduly delay play" clause. They contended that any practice putting during the matches was "undue delay," even though they made that decision months before the first ball was struck. There was no doubt this was a bend of the rules, but as the Committee,

When Sam Torrence and Curtis Strange agreed on no practice putting during the Ryder Cup matches, it illustrated the complexities and vagaries of the rules. JAMIE SQUIRE/ALL SPORT

Torrence and Strange could make those kinds of discretionary decisions.

Perhaps the most important rules in the final section of the rule book are the last two, 33 and 34, which outline the powers and responsibilities of the Committee, and what a player's rights are in settling disputes and questions. The final section of the rule book, **Rule 34-3**, reads as follows:

In the absence of a referee, any dispute or doubtful point on the Rules shall be referred to the Committee, whose decision shall be final.

If the Committee cannot come to a decision, it shall refer the dispute or doubtful point to the Rules of Golf Committee of the United States Golf Association, whose decision shall be final.

If the dispute or doubtful point has not been referred to the Rules of Golf Committee, the player or players have the right to refer an agreed statement through the Secretary of the Club to the Rules of Golf Committee for an opinion as to the correctness of the decision given. The reply will be sent to the Secretary of the Club or Clubs concerned.

If play is conducted other than in accordance with the Rules of Golf, the Rules of Golf Committee will not give a decision on any question.

The preceding pages don't come close to covering all the quirky rules and rulings that have taken place in golf throughout the years. For that you'd need several volumes of dictionary length, the kinds of books measured by weight instead of pages. But the one thing all the rulings outlined here have in common is the underlying honesty and integrity of those involved.

No question in golf should go unasked, and no controversy concerning our rules should go unanswered. That's what makes golf the greatest game in the world. Whether it's Tiger Woods, Phil Mickelson, or David Duval asking the question, or you and your buddies after a friendly Saturday match, the answer you get will be the same. That's why golf doesn't need an officiating crew. The honor and pride we all take in our game keep us honest, and keep the game fair for all who play it.

AFTERWORD

Golf is more than a game for me; it's a love affair I've carried on for more than sixty years. During that time, I don't think anyone has been more devoted to the integrity of the game and the growth of golf than I. For over thirty years I've been a spokesman for the USGA, encouraging ordinary golfers—men, women, and kids across America—to join their national association to help preserve, protect, and grow our game. Like every other cause I've ever taken on, I believed what I said in those USGA ads. And despite what some may think, I still do.

In the latter part of 2000, I found myself in the middle of a controversy with the USGA that I didn't want or expect. I sure wasn't looking for a fight, and I never thought my views on something as insignificant as metal-headed drivers could create such uproar. I'm sorry that such a controversy ensued. However, as long as there is golf, there will be some differences of opinion about the rules of the game.

At the core of this dispute is what I feel is a flawed premise that today's club-making technology has added a great amount of distance to the game, so much so, in fact, that many classic golf courses in America are becoming obsolete pitch-and-putt tracts. Today's players hit the ball too far, the argument goes, and it is the job of the USGA to curtail that trend. I think there are several ways this could be accomplished. To my mind, one of the best ways of doing this would be to rein in the golf ball, something I've advocated for a long time.

A lot of highly trained specialists disagreed with the USGA's new standard dealing with this situation, some terming it arbitrary and capricious. The result of the back-and-forth of the debate was a growing "us" versus "them" division between the USGA and the citizen golfers who make up their 800,000-plus membership ranks. I like to think that I played a small role in helping the USGA build that membership, so this bothered me.

In making their case, the USGA and its advocates cited the large gains in driving distance. In my judgment, this is easily explained. Besides the "longer" balls, we have stronger, fitter athletes playing in the top levels of the game, and there have been tremendous advances in agronomy and course maintenance practices that are far better than they have ever been before. Physics is the great equalizer in golf. A few added yards are meaningless if you just hit the ball deeper into the rough.

I was one of the last players to switch from wood to metal composite heads, and that change points up a mistake, or shall we call it an omission, by the game's ruling bodies when they allowed the size of the heads to be increased immeasurably.

Then, when the R&A declined to legislate against the new crop of drivers, the game worldwide suddenly had two sets of rules, one for the United States and Mexico, where golf is governed by the USGA, and the other for the rest of the world

under the R&A. For instance, a player from America who quali-
fies for the Open Championship or British Amateur could use any
driver that he chooses in those competitions, but doesn't have
the same options back home.

Months after the conflicting rules had gone into effect, the
USGA's position was dealt a blow when, at the Open Championship at St. Andrews, the best players in the world competed on
the oldest golf course in the world and nobody made it obsolete.
Then, in late summer of 2001, I saw another telling sign. During
the Battle at Bighorn, a prime-time televised foursome match
involving Tiger Woods, Annika Sorenstam, David Duval, and
Karrie Webb, both Tiger and David played a 237-yard par-three
with 7-irons, hitting their tee shots over the green and into the
back bunker. Sure, the hole was slightly downhill and downwind,
but both players hit 7-irons more than 235 yards. Think of that!
Today's players just hit the ball farther than anybody could have
ever imagined. They could play most golf courses with nothing
longer than a 5-iron and still shoot below par, I assure you.

Let's look at what has happened on the European PGA Tour
over two seasons of play under R&A rules. There have been no
threats to the game, nobody has made courses obsolete, scores
haven't plummeted below 60, and none of the ancient links
courses on the Open Championship rota are about to be dropped
for that reason. Sure, a few courses have added yardage over the
years, but the same thing happened when steel shafts replaced
hickory and when irrigation systems and gas-powered mowers
were first introduced in golf.

Obviously, the rules of golf are being altered based on the
potential of the young people coming into the game. Times have

changed in that regard. When I was an amateur and thinking about turning pro, I had to keep those thoughts to myself. All you had to do then was get caught saying you were considering a pro career and, presto, you were a pro in the eyes of the rules makers. Nowadays, the rules define professionalism as "receiving payment or compensation for serving as a professional golfer or identifying oneself as a professional golfer" and/or "taking any action for the purpose of becoming a professional golfer." Yet, we still see cases in which, if a local businessman or well-to-do citizen is willing to foot the bill for travel, room, and board for a youngster to play in a tournament away from home when the parents can't afford it, the boy or girl would forfeit amateur status if he accepted that generosity. This certainly doesn't threaten the integrity of the game, nor does the common practice of a foursome agreeing to take mulligans off the first tee, even though it violates the strict interpretation of the rules. If you want to take a mulligan and still post a score in the handicap book after the round, your buddies might have a problem, but I don't.

I'm sure that I could watch the golfers at one of my clubs for a while on any given day and be able to disqualify half of them for this or that infraction. But why would I want to? Golf should be fun. And those of us who love the game should be encouraging fun and recreation, not building roadblocks for future golfing generations.

I hate having two sets of rules for our game, and I hope that the situation changes very soon. But it's not a crisis and we shouldn't treat it as such. Golf will survive as it always has. Beginners and pros alike will continue to make mistakes on the course that will cost them penalties in accordance with the rules, and viewers of tournaments at home will continue to phone in every time they see something untoward during Sunday telecasts.

The USGA and R&A will continue to massage and modify the rules as situations warrant, and club and ball manufacturers will continue to make products to help players enjoy golf and shoot better scores. As for me, I'll continue to play and practice golf, working on clubs in my workshop, having fun playing with my pals, and speaking my mind when I think it's appropriate, especially in my efforts not to let unnecessary regulations stifle the growth of the game. I can do little else. I love golf, and as long as that love burns inside me, I will continue to speak out for what I think is right and just and good in our game.

Let me reiterate: The ruling bodies of golf must get together and do what we all know has to be done—agree on one set of rules for all of golf.

INDEX

Aaron, Tommy, 50, 51
abnormal ground conditions, 201–8
Accenture Match Play Championship, 22
advice, 61–65
aggregate scoring, 154–55
Alfred Dunhill Cup:
    (1996), 126
    (2000), 221–23
Alfred Dunhill Masters, 190–92
Allan, Brian, 192
alligators, 19
all square, 22
alternate shot, 230–32
Andy Williams San Diego Open (1987), 101
animals, burrowing, 201–2, 205
ants, 202
Aoki, Isao, 104, 105
Arizona Mid-Amateur (2000), 44, 46–47
artificial devices, 114, 189
AT&T Pebble Beach National Pro-Am, 204, 205, 210
Australian Wills Masters (1964), 82, 84
Azinger, Paul, 102, 103, 104, 185, 186

Baddeley, Aaron, 169
Ballesteros, Seve, 65, 171, 172
balls:
    cleaning, 125–26, 128, 175–76
    damaged, 40
    embedded, 26–27
    falling off tee, 80
    in hazards, 88–89
    identifying, 86–89, 119, 215, 219, 226
    inchworming, 128, 130

influencing position or movement of, 12–14
balls: (cont.)
    interfering with or assisting play, 177–79
    lift, clean, and place, 91–92, 204–5
    lifting, 126
    lifting, dropping, placing, 165–74
    longer, 238
    lost, 82, 89, 206, 208, 215–24
    marking, 97, 125, 128, 178–79
    marking position of, 166–68
    in motion, deflected or stopped, 157–64
    moved by outside agency, 147–48
    nonconforming, 40
    out of bounds, 215–24
    overhanging lip of hole, 134, 136, 139–40
    playing as it lies, 91–110
    prototype, 40
    provisional (second), 119, 210, 215–16, 221–23, 226
    replacing, 119, 123, 153–54
    at rest, moved, 147–55
    searching for, 81–89
    snatched by dog, 147–48
    striking, 111–18
    in trees, 82, 84, 86
    unplayable-lie, 86, 225–28
    wrong, 24, 89, 119–23, 210
Baton Rouge Open (1960), 151, 153
Bay Hill Invitational, 206

(1988), 18–19
(2001), 154–55
Bean, Andy, 155
Beman, Deane, 37
Benson and Hedges International Open (2000), 52–53
Betzler, Ken, 86
Bing Crosby Clambake, 204, 210, 223
Bjorn, Thomas, 120
Blalock, Jane, 128, 129, 130
Bob Hope Chrysler Classic, (2001), 34
Bolt, Tommy, 136, 137
Bradley, Pat, 74–76, 76
British Open Championship:
    (1960), 193–95
    (1974), 195–96
    (1998), 218–19, 221
    (2001), 1, 35–37
    Senior (2001), 120
Bro, Betsy, 23–24
Browne, Olin, 86, 87
building a stance, 101
Burnet Senior Clasic (1995), 58, 60
burrowing animals, 201–2, 205
Burton, Brandie, 74
butterfly, waving away, 183, 184
Byrne, Miles, 35

caddies:
    holding umbrella, 113
    number of, 44, 46–47
    position of, 113
    as witnesses, 69–70
Campbell, Hugh, 36
Campbell, Michael, 192
Casper, Billy, 224
casual water, 201, 202, 205–6, 208